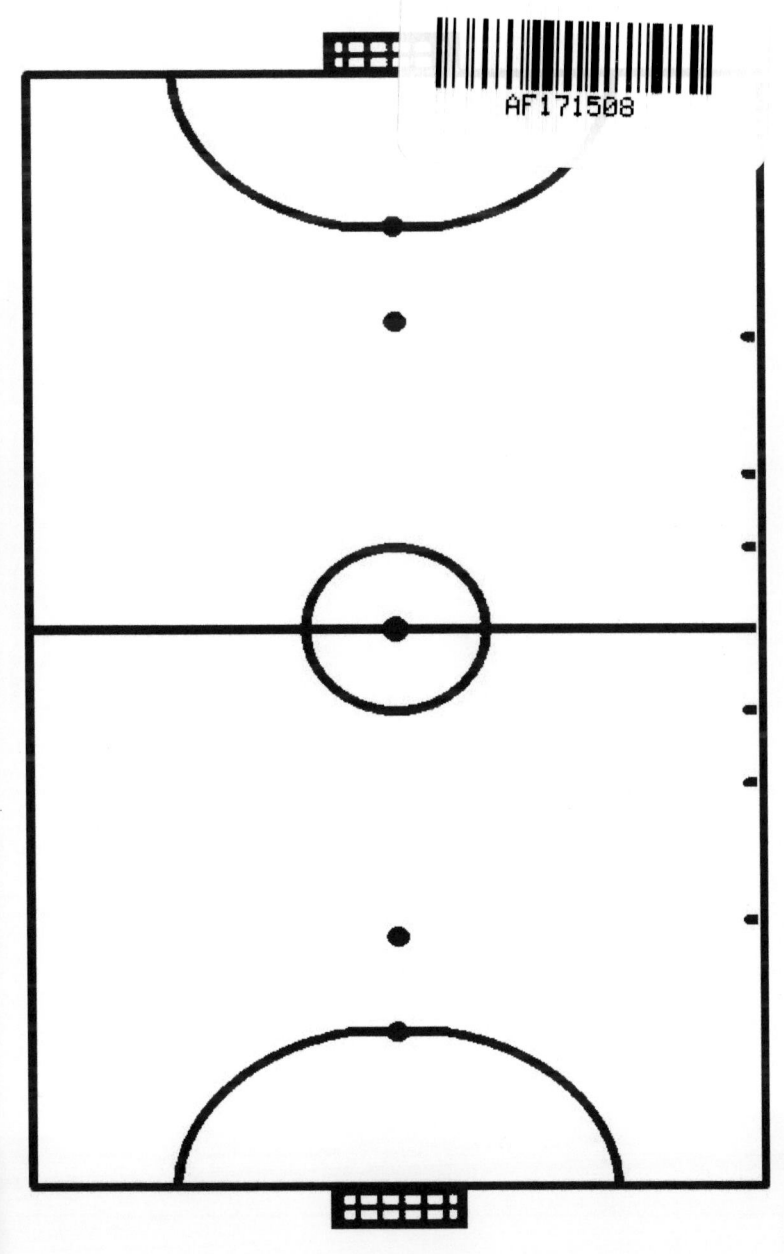

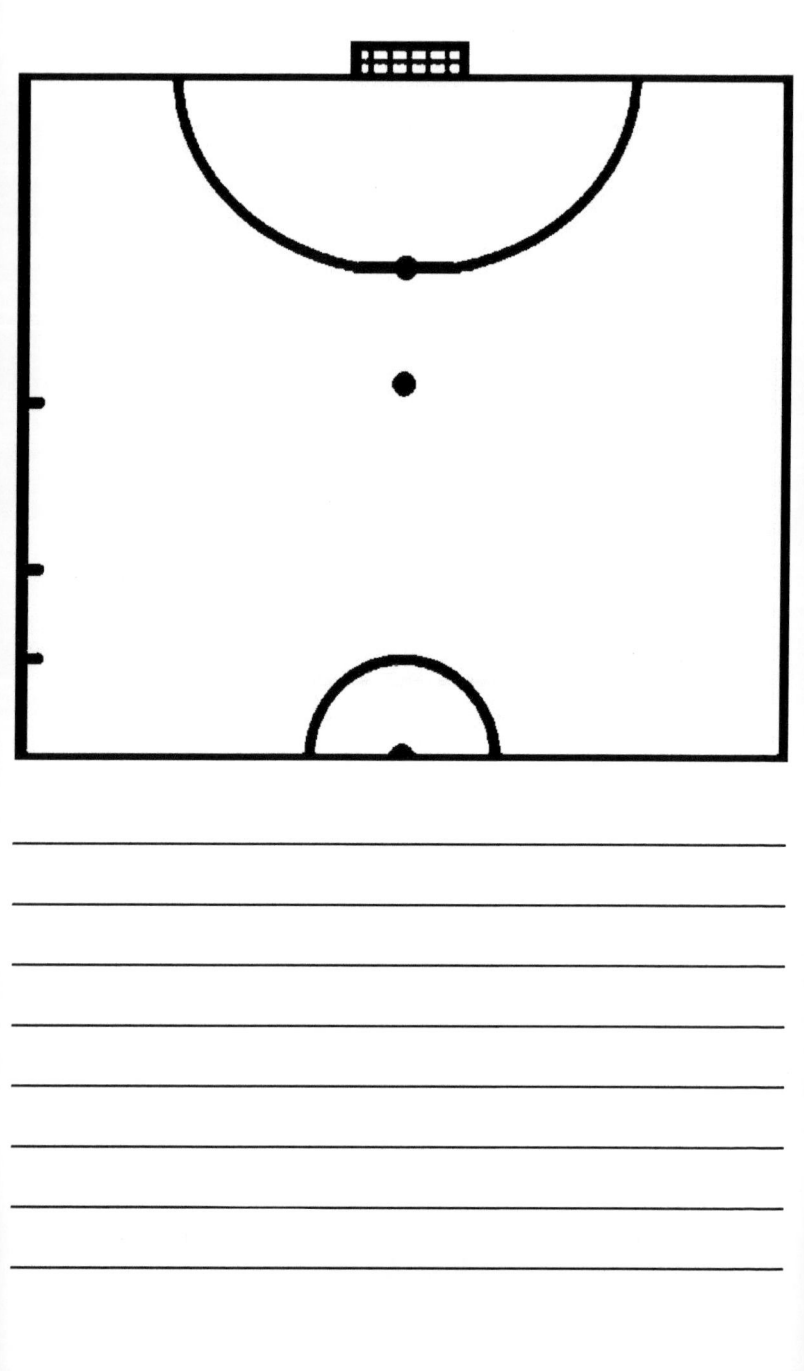

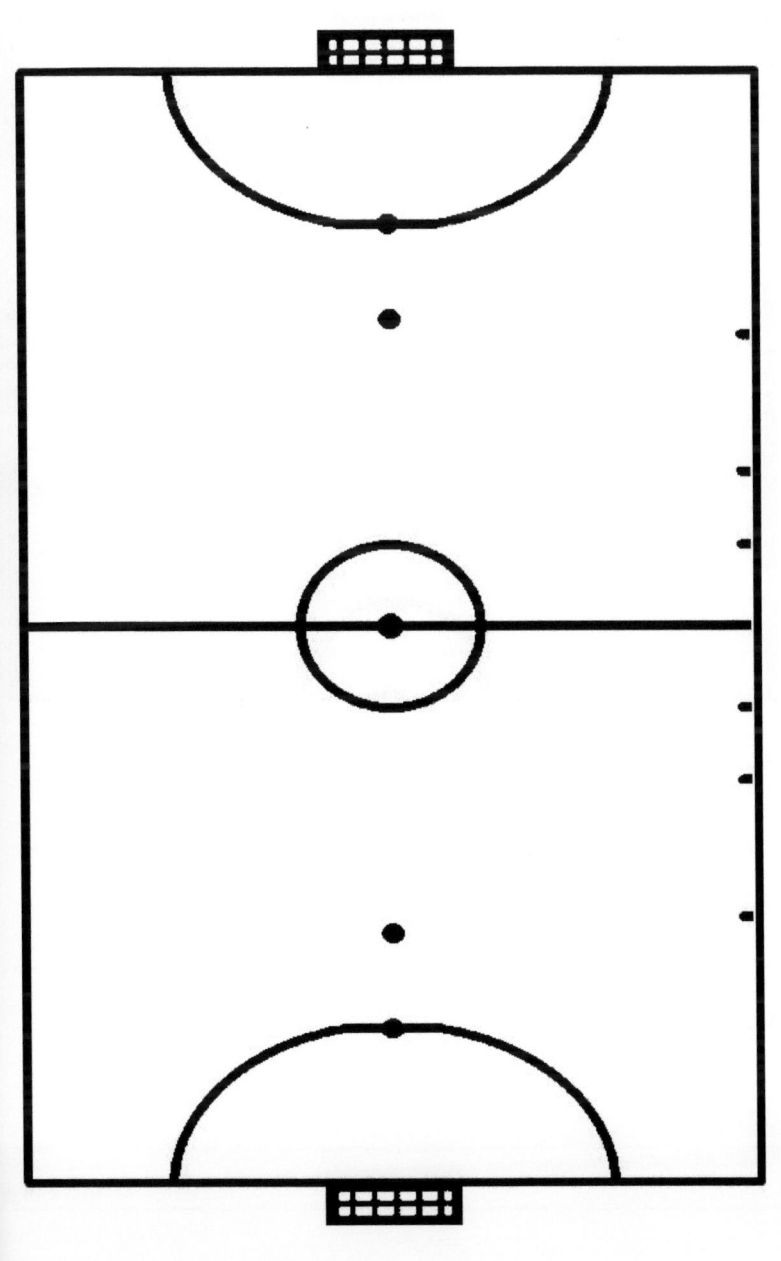

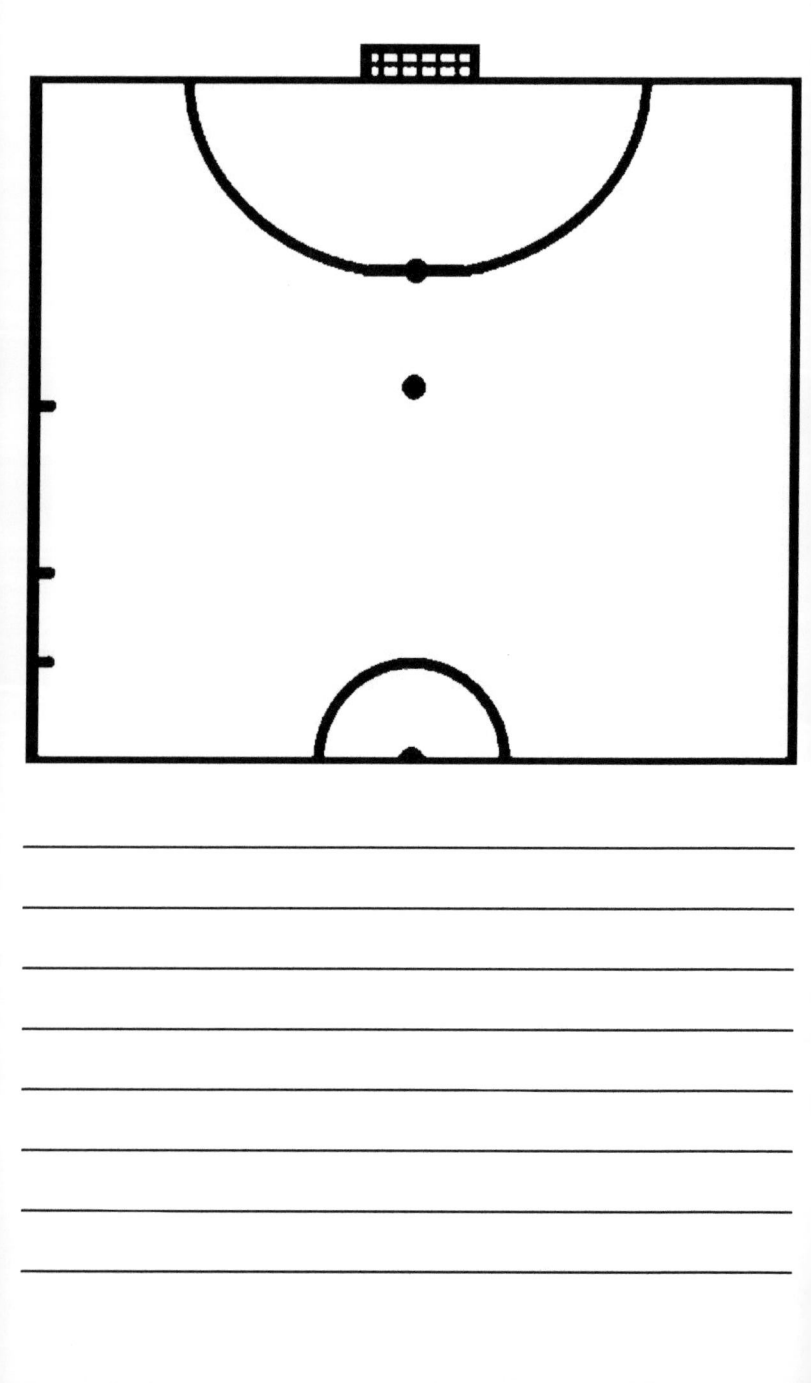

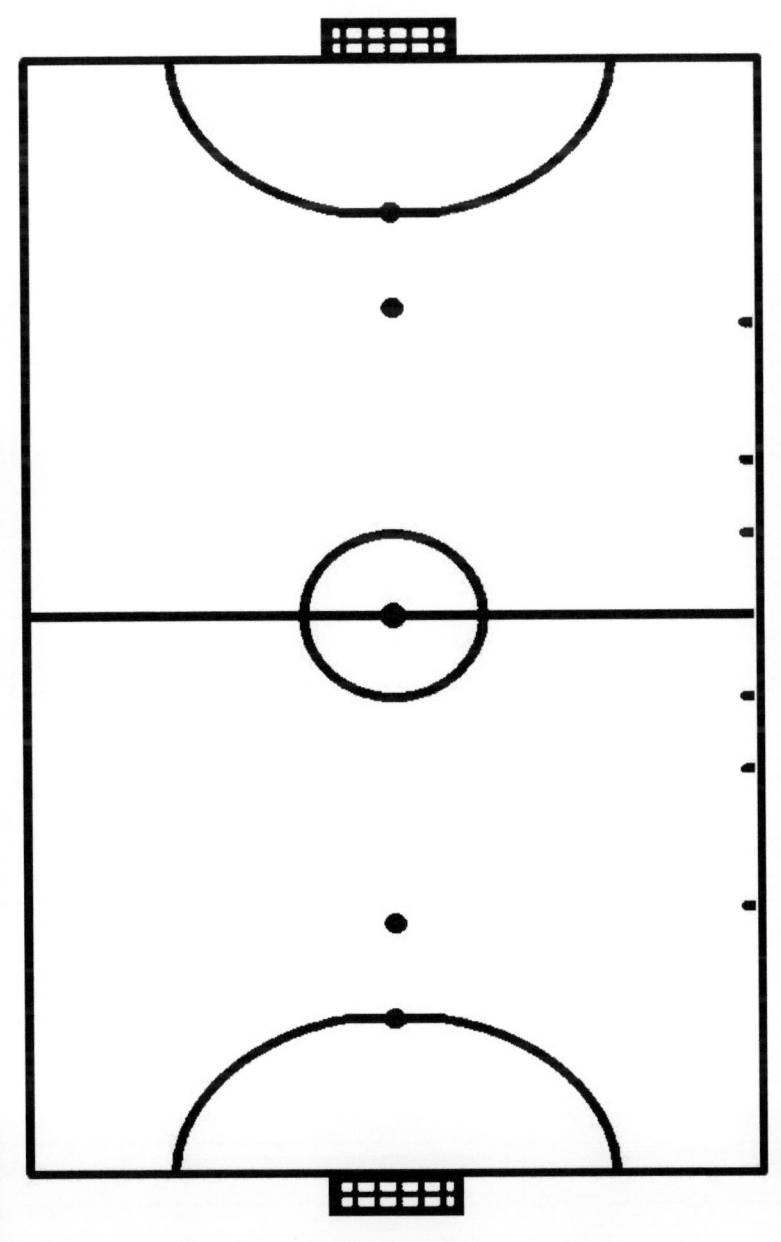

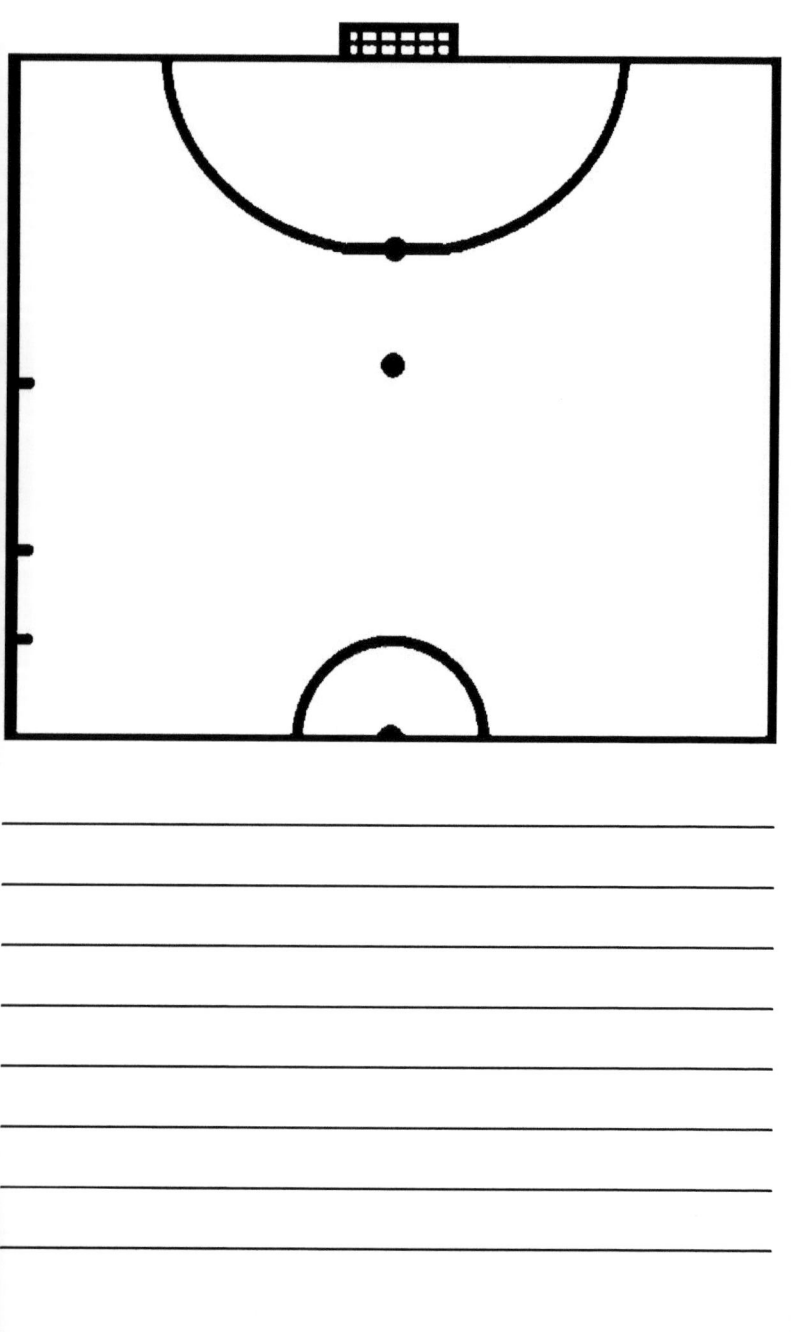

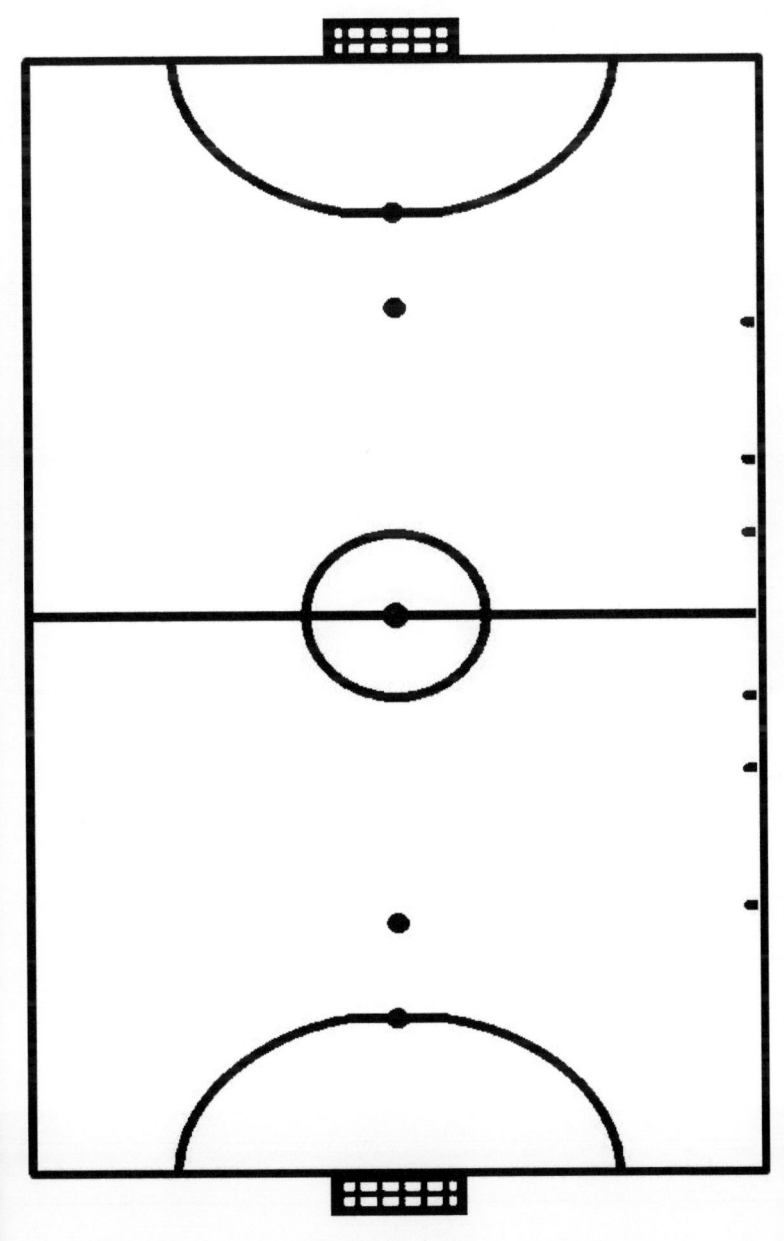

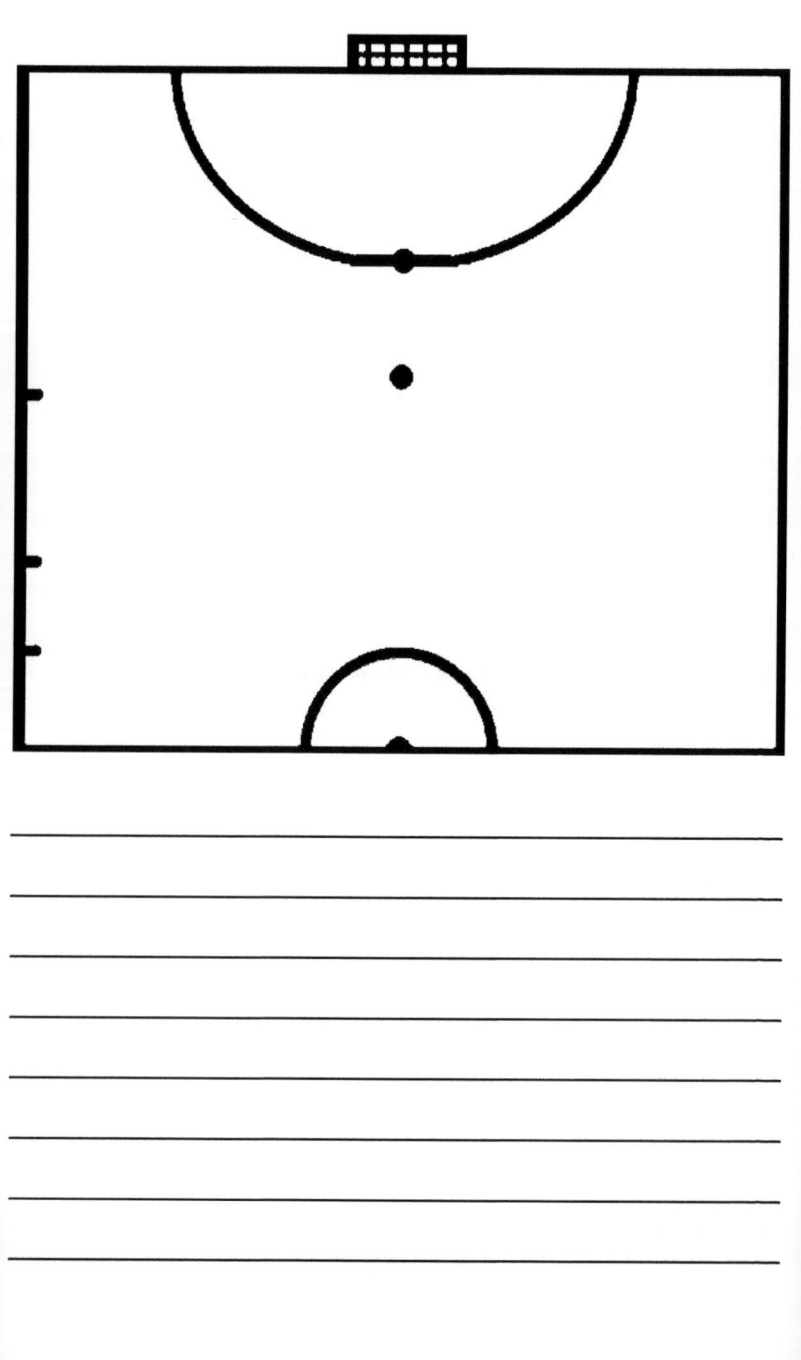

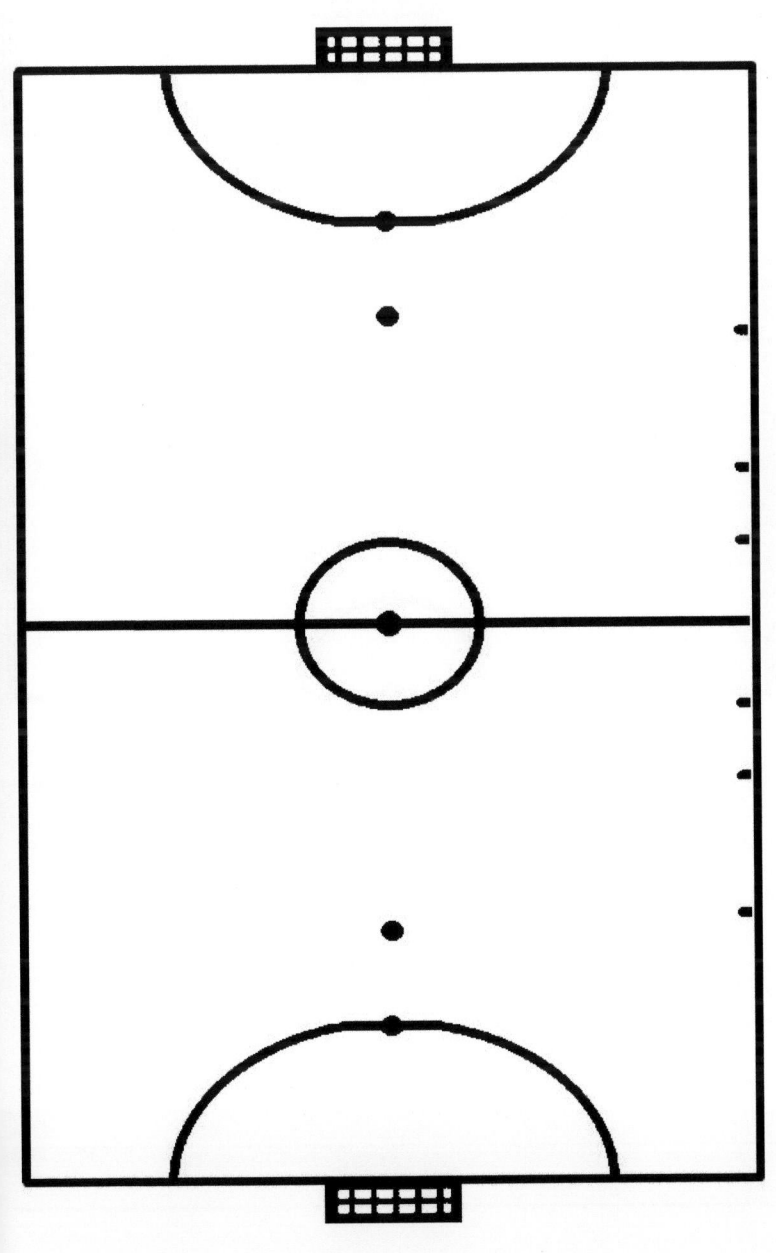

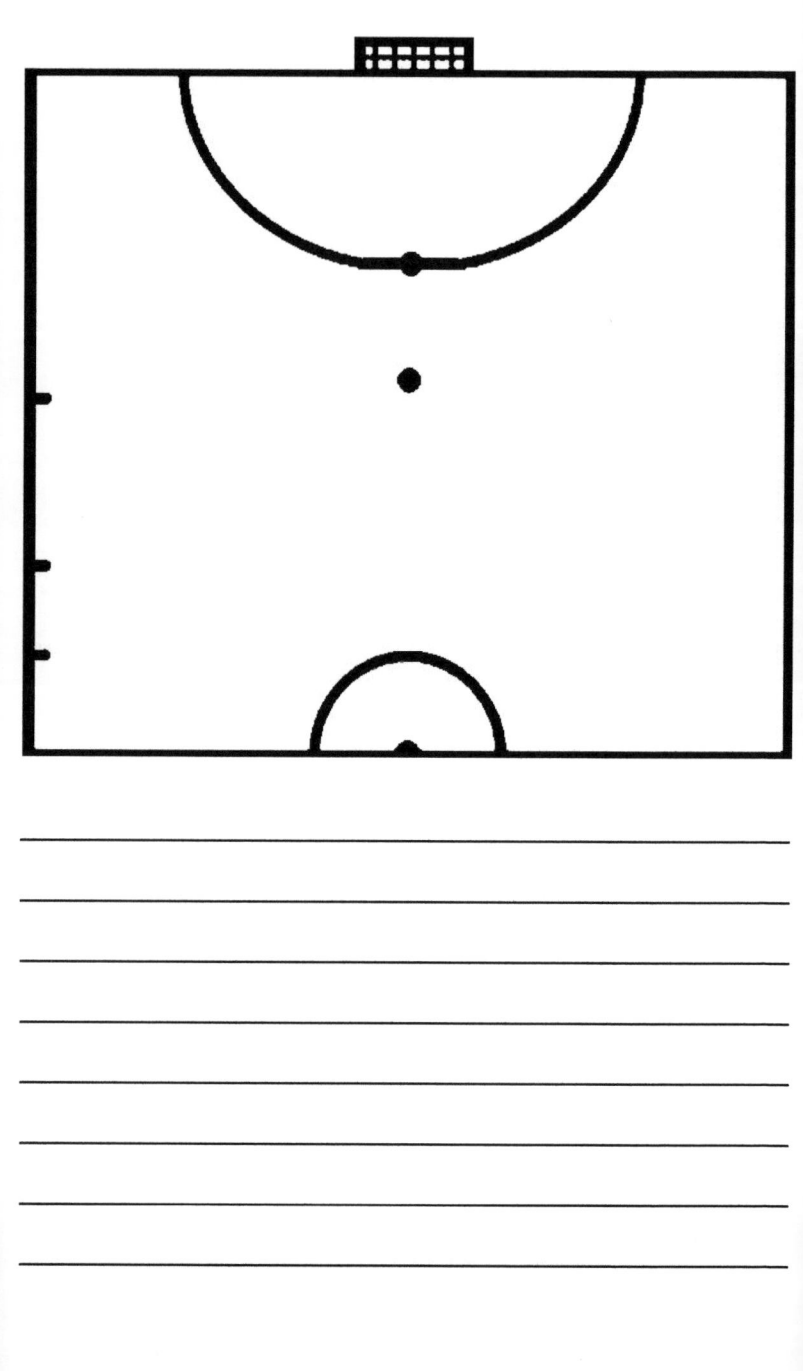

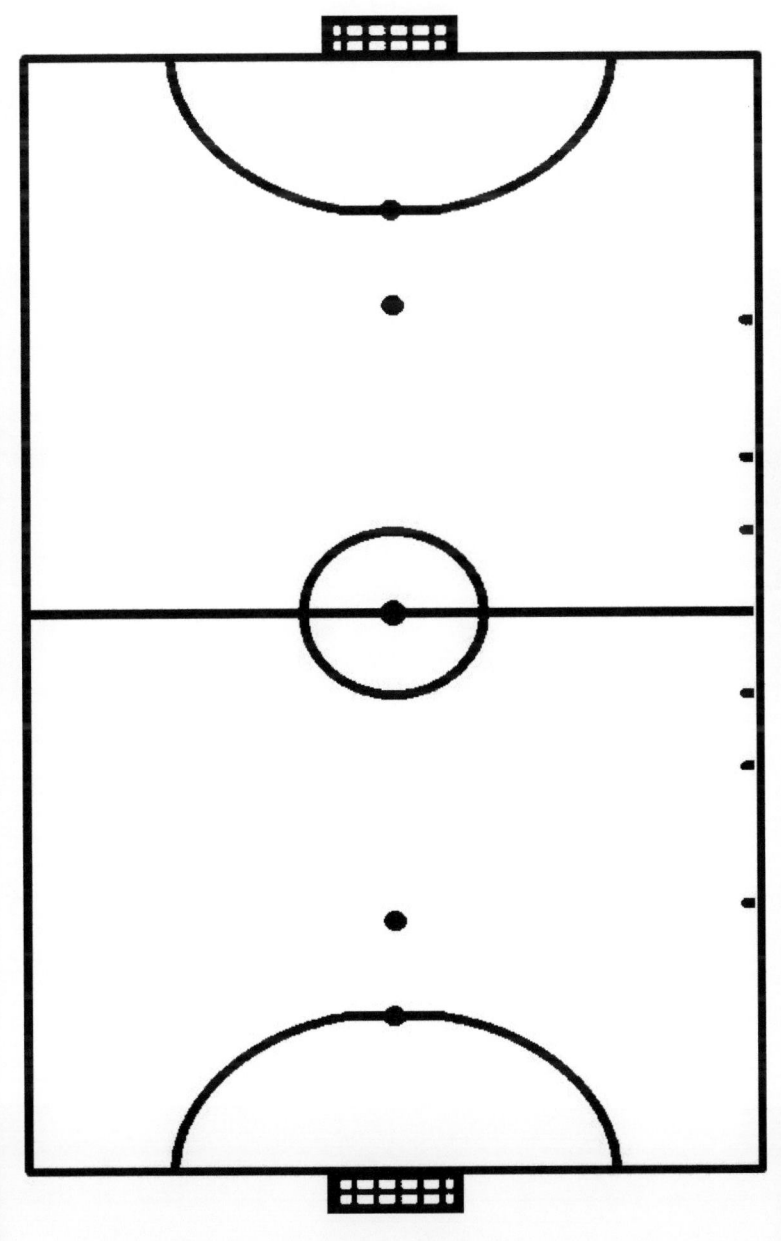

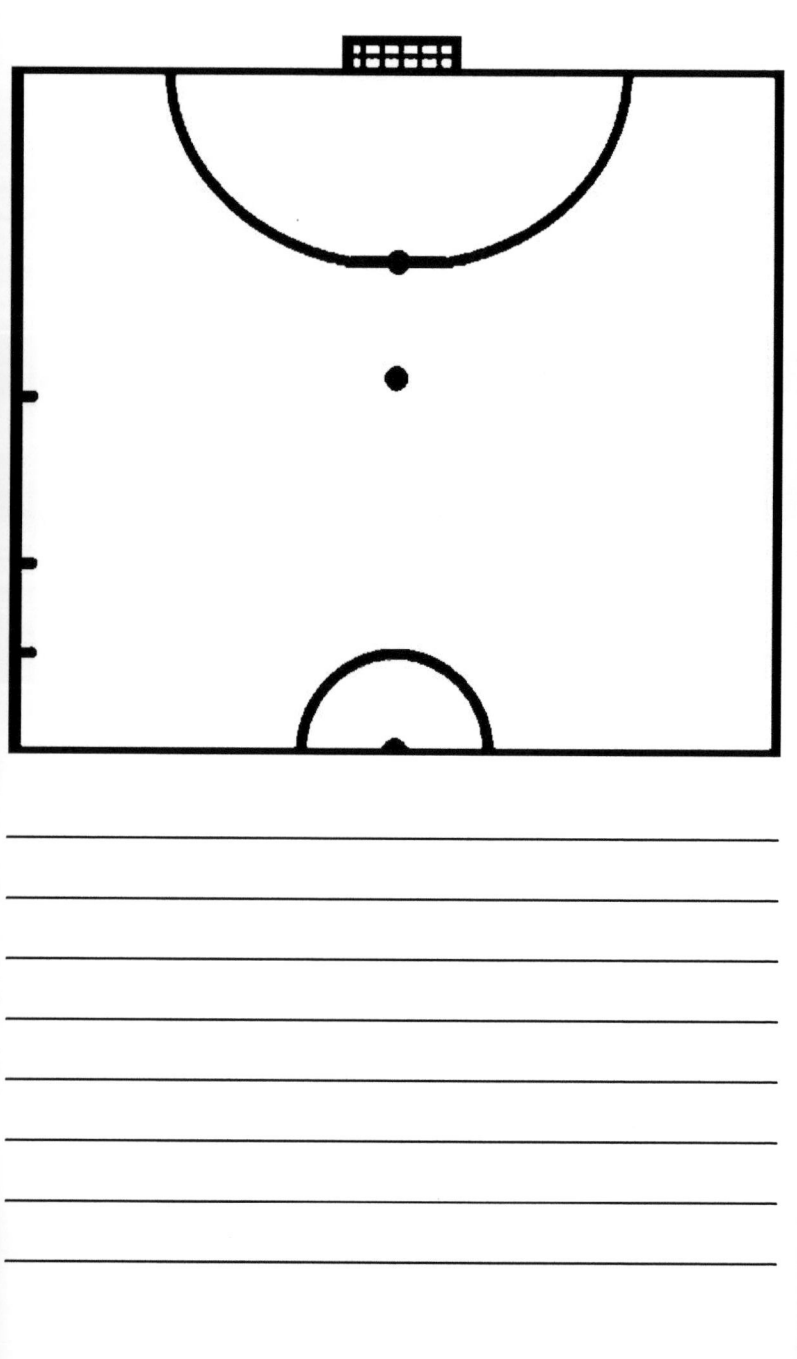

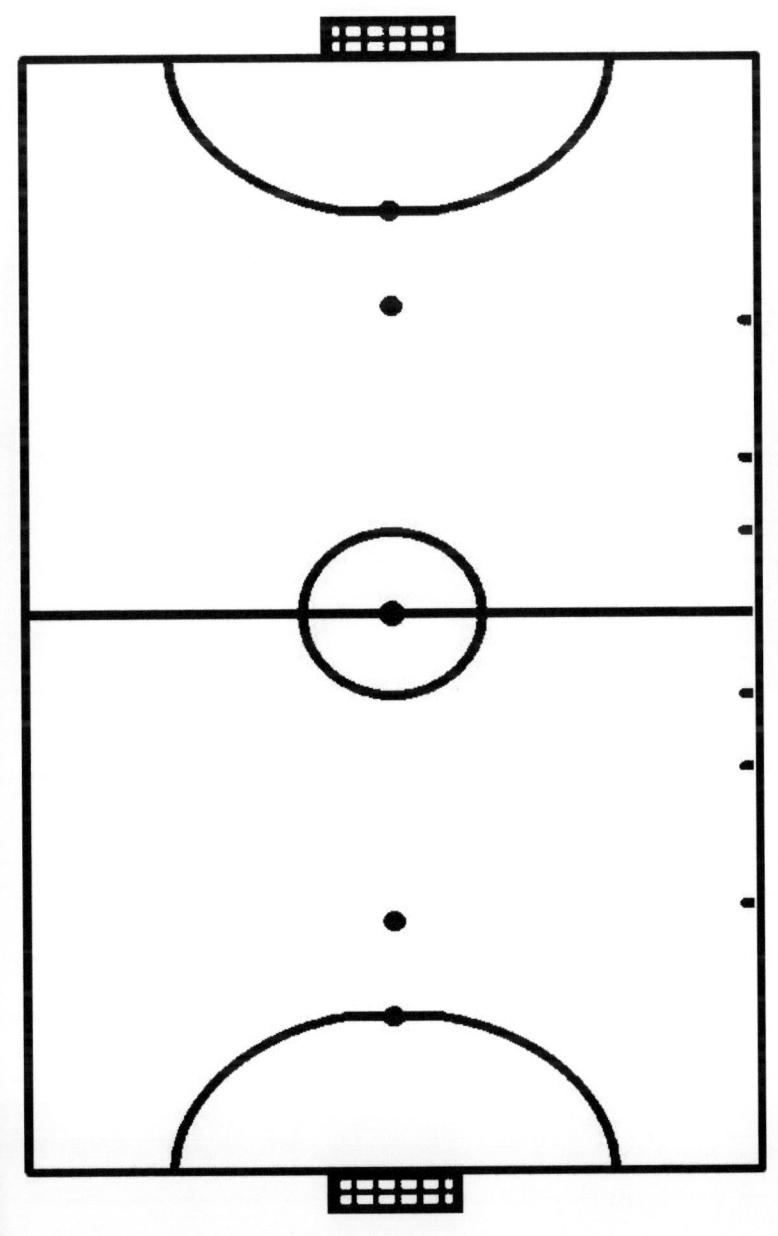

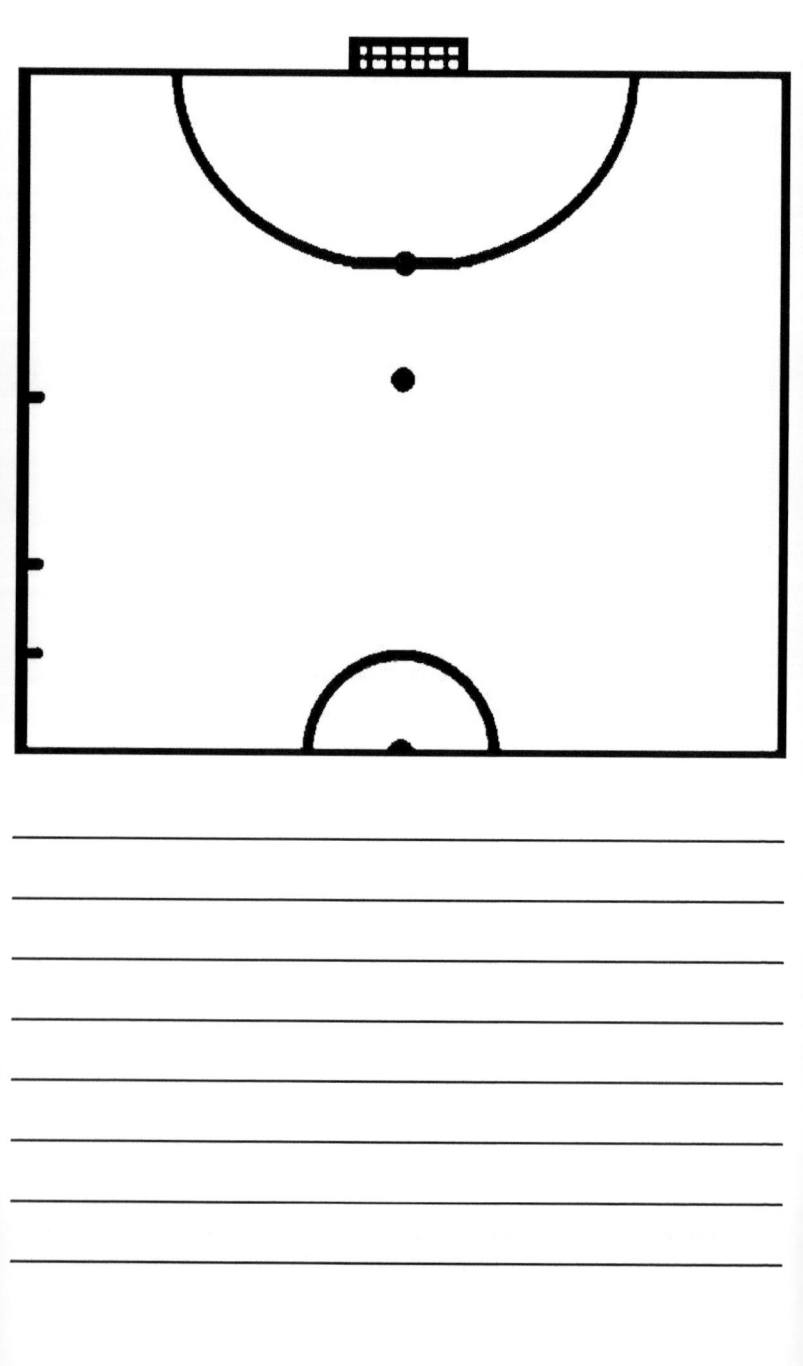

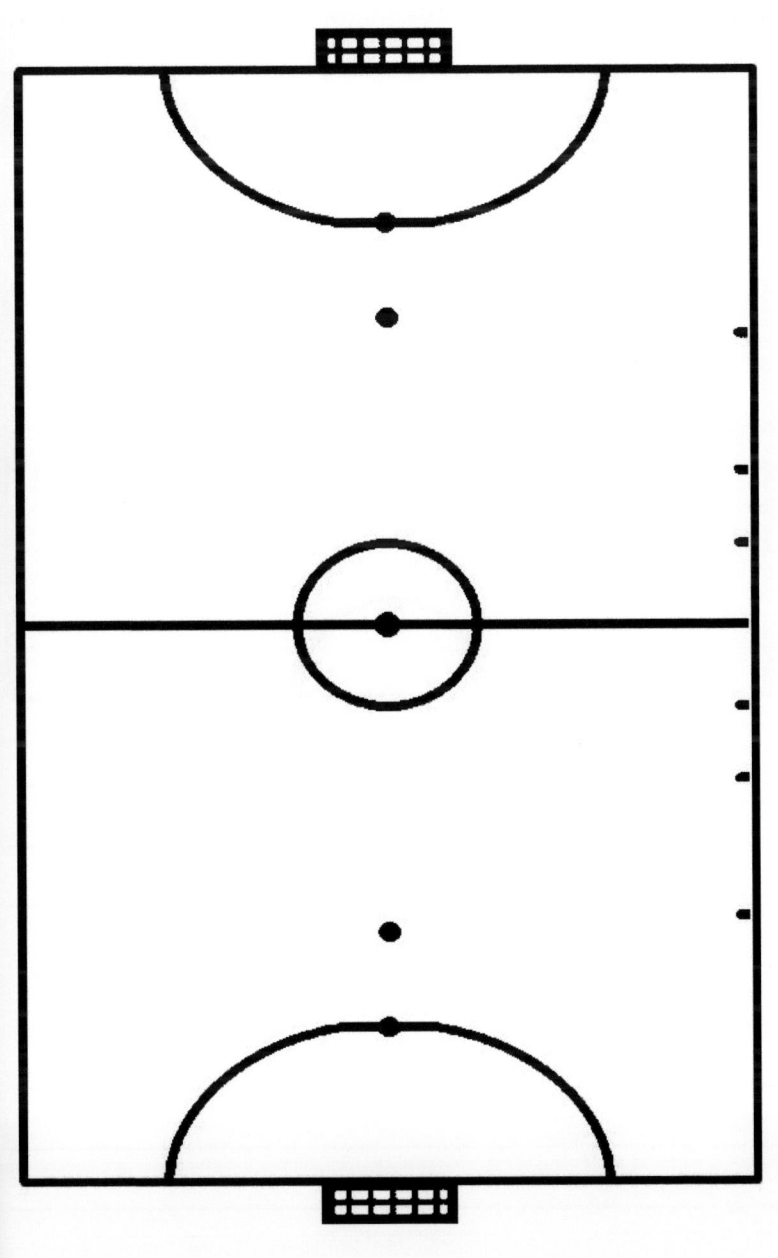

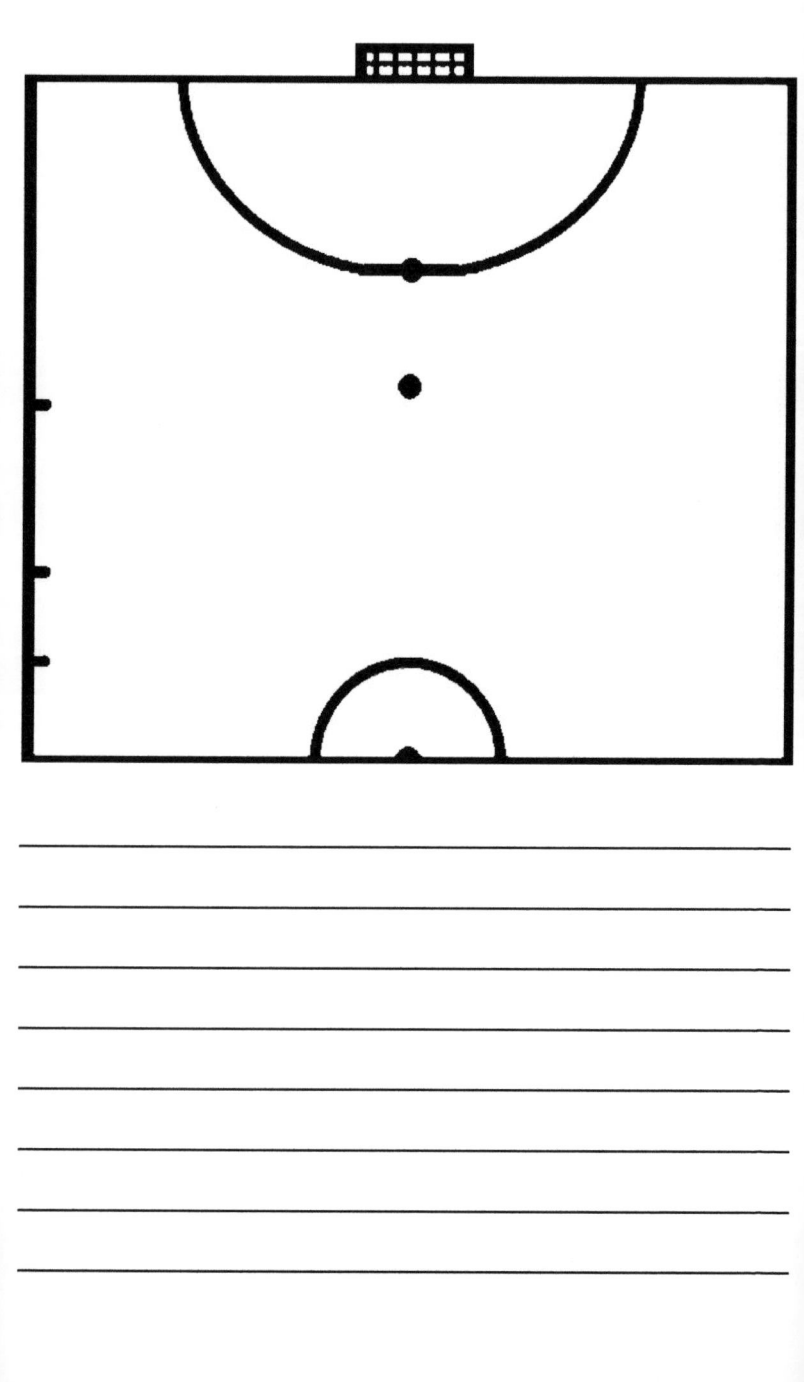

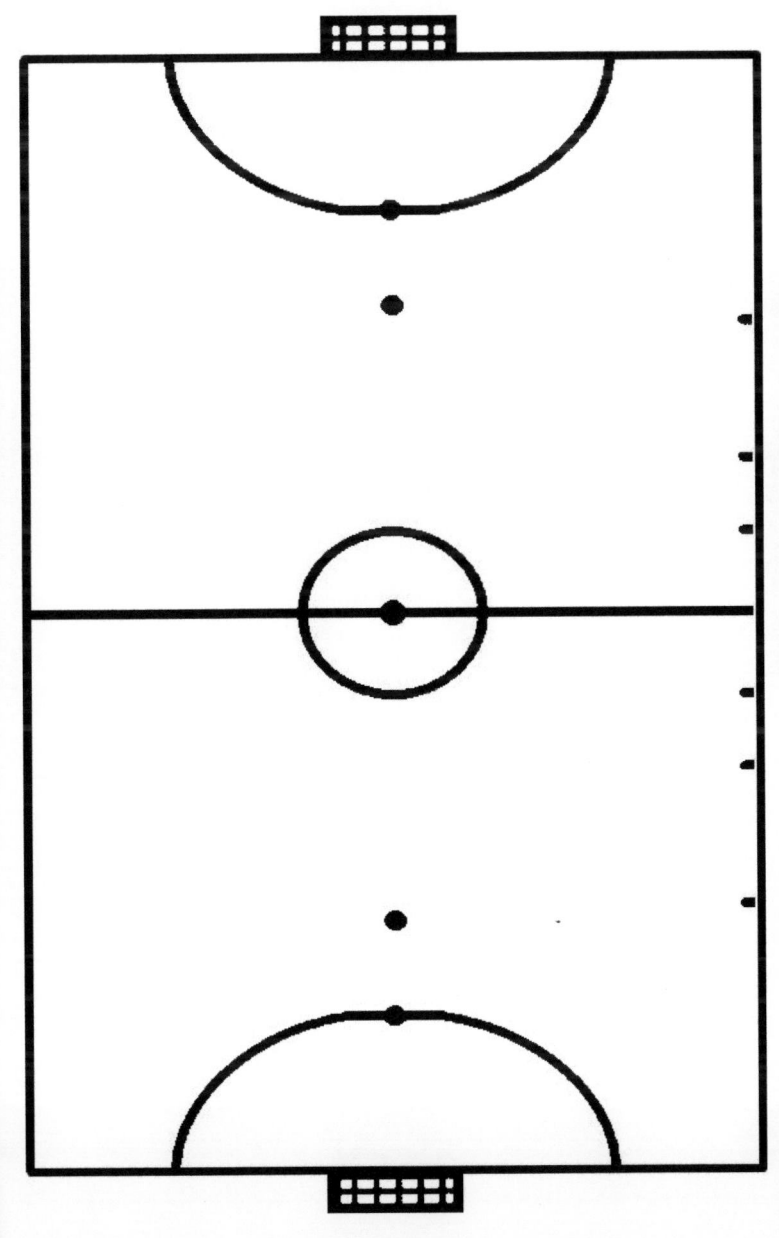

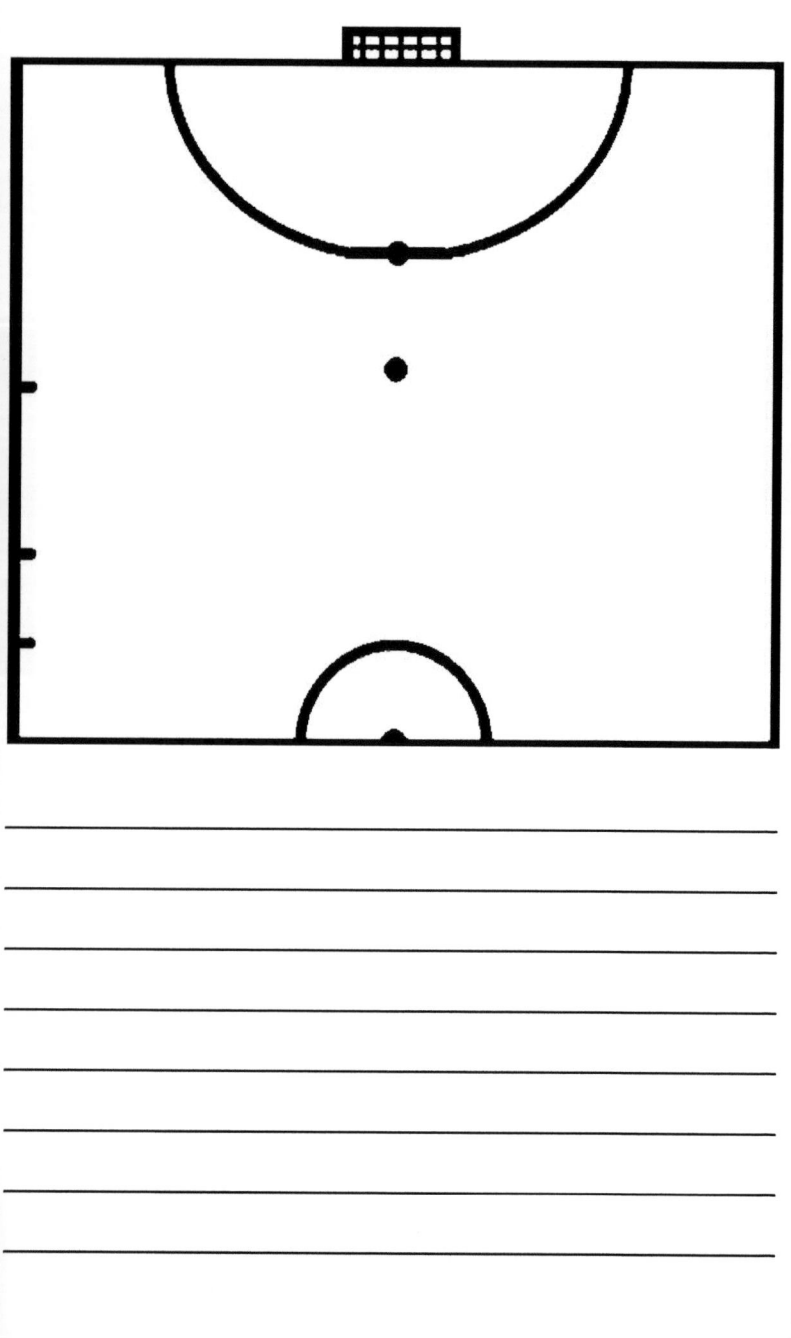

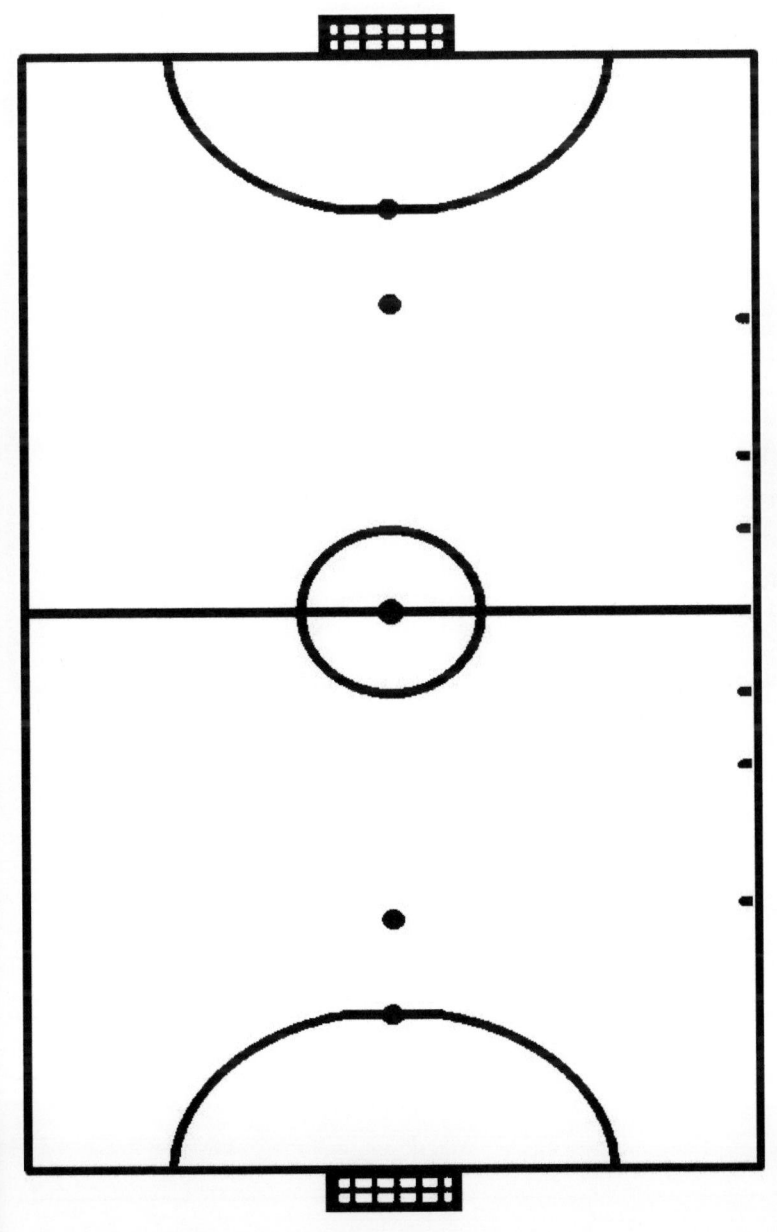

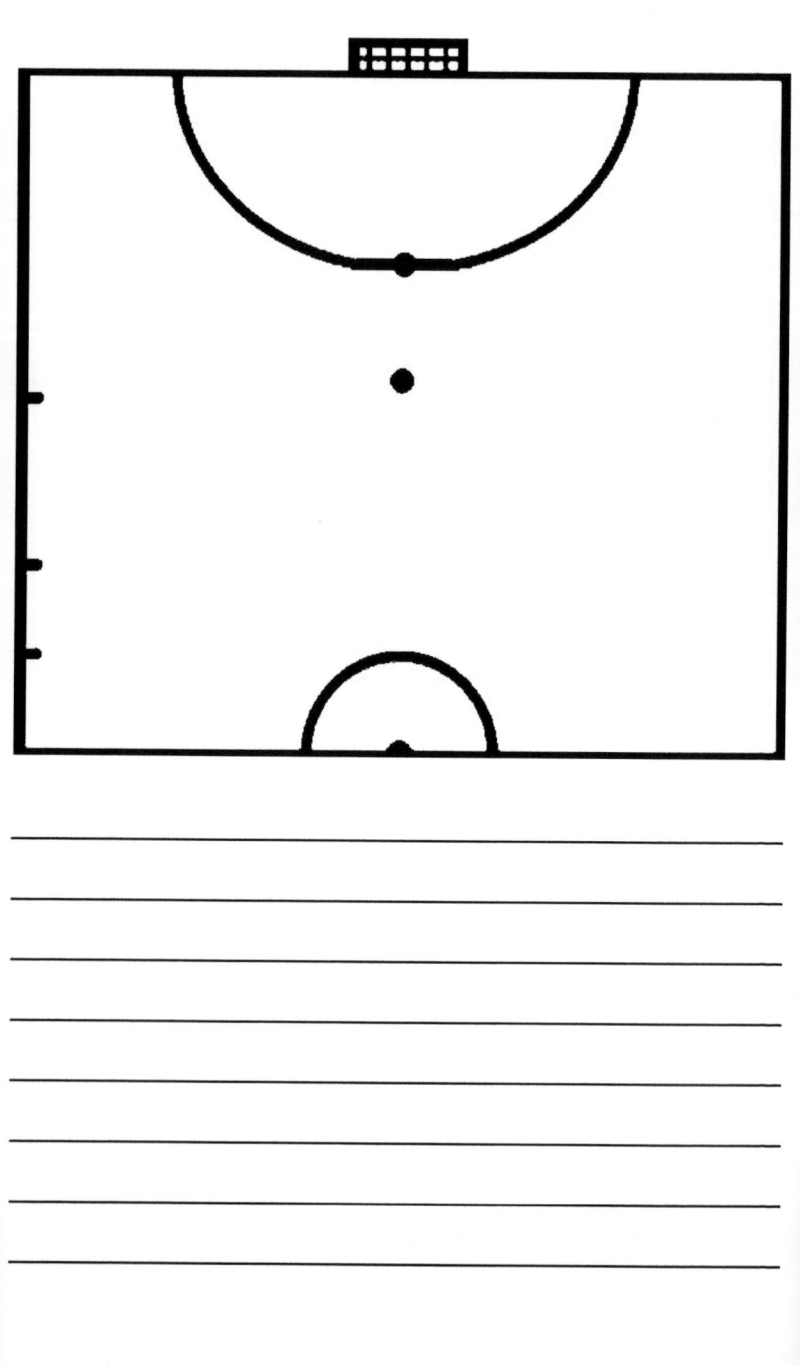

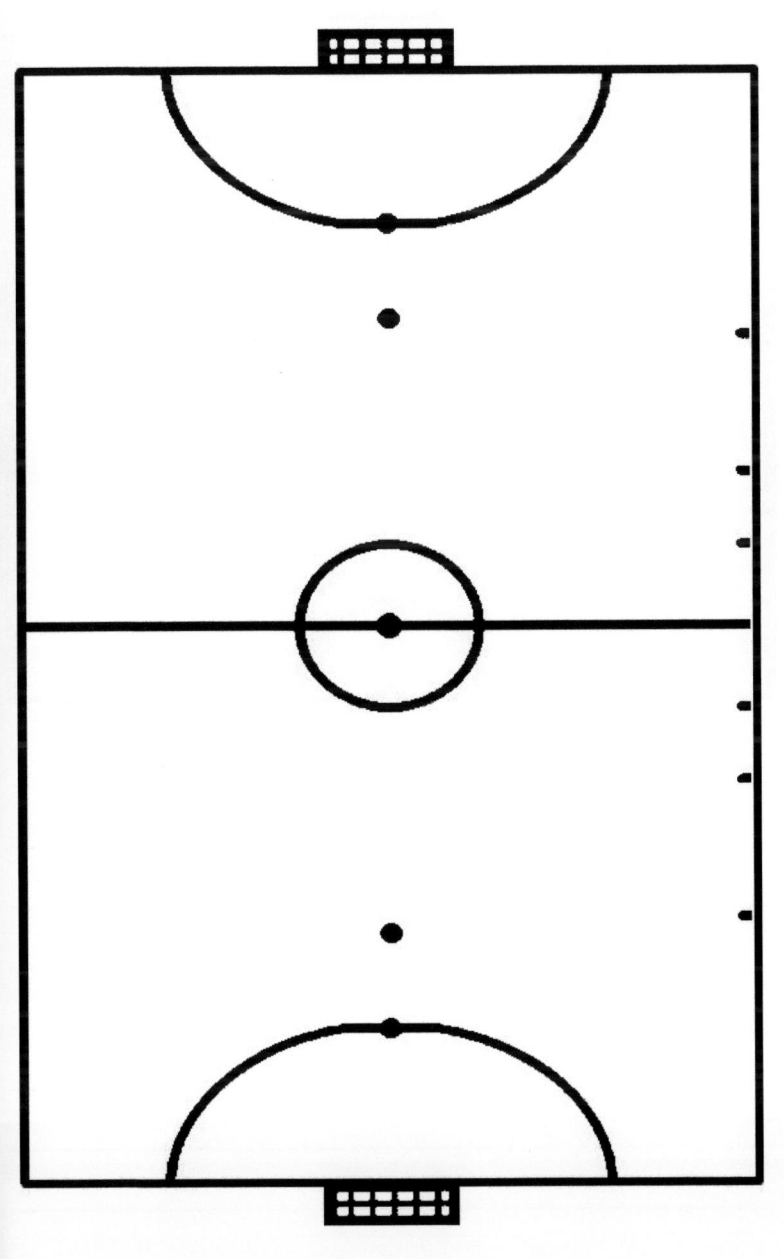

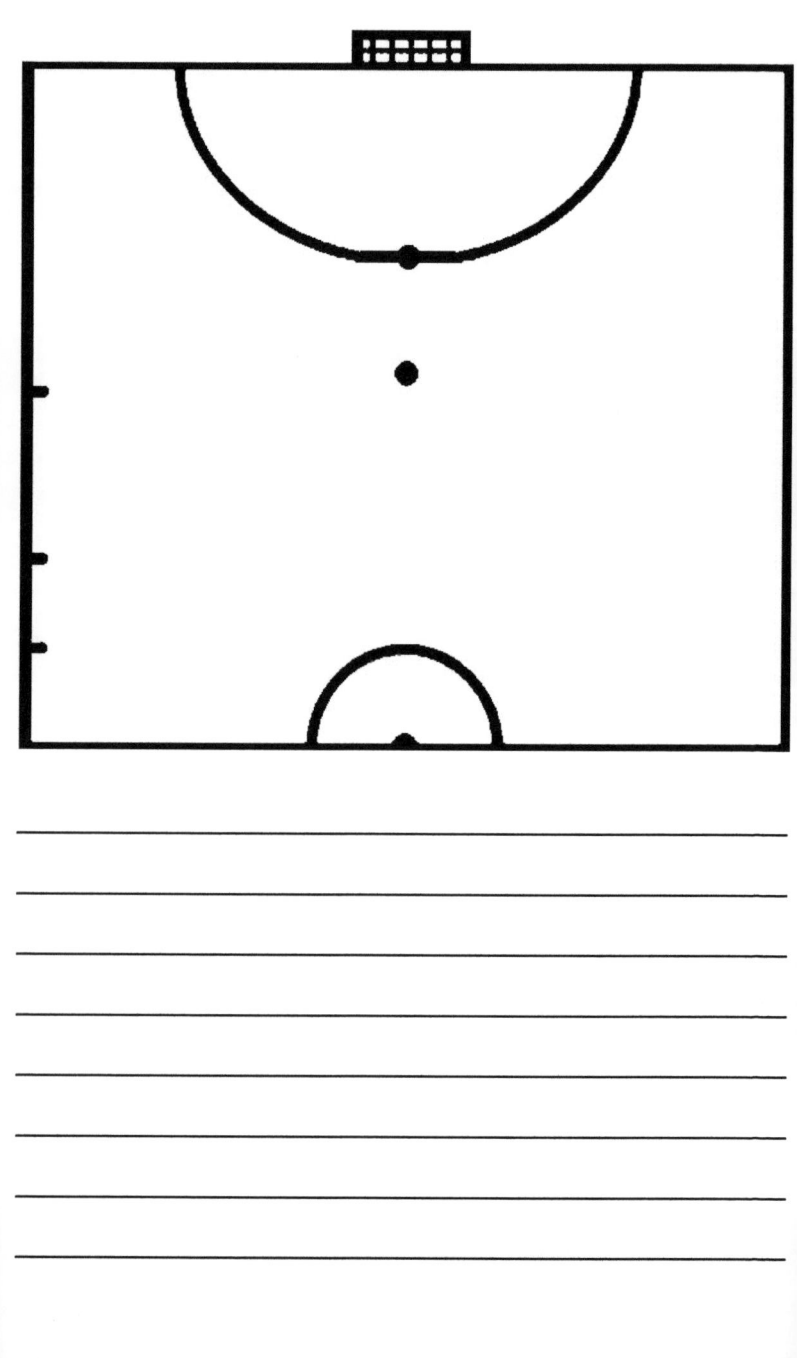

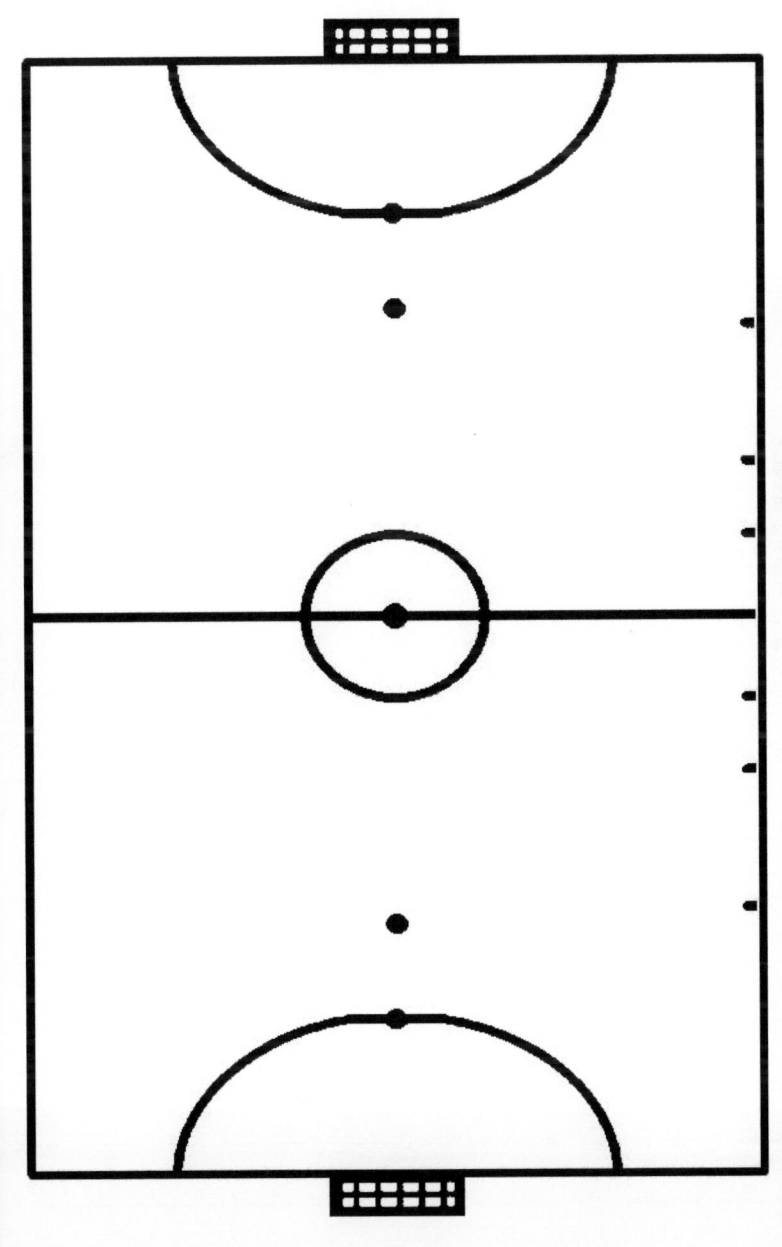

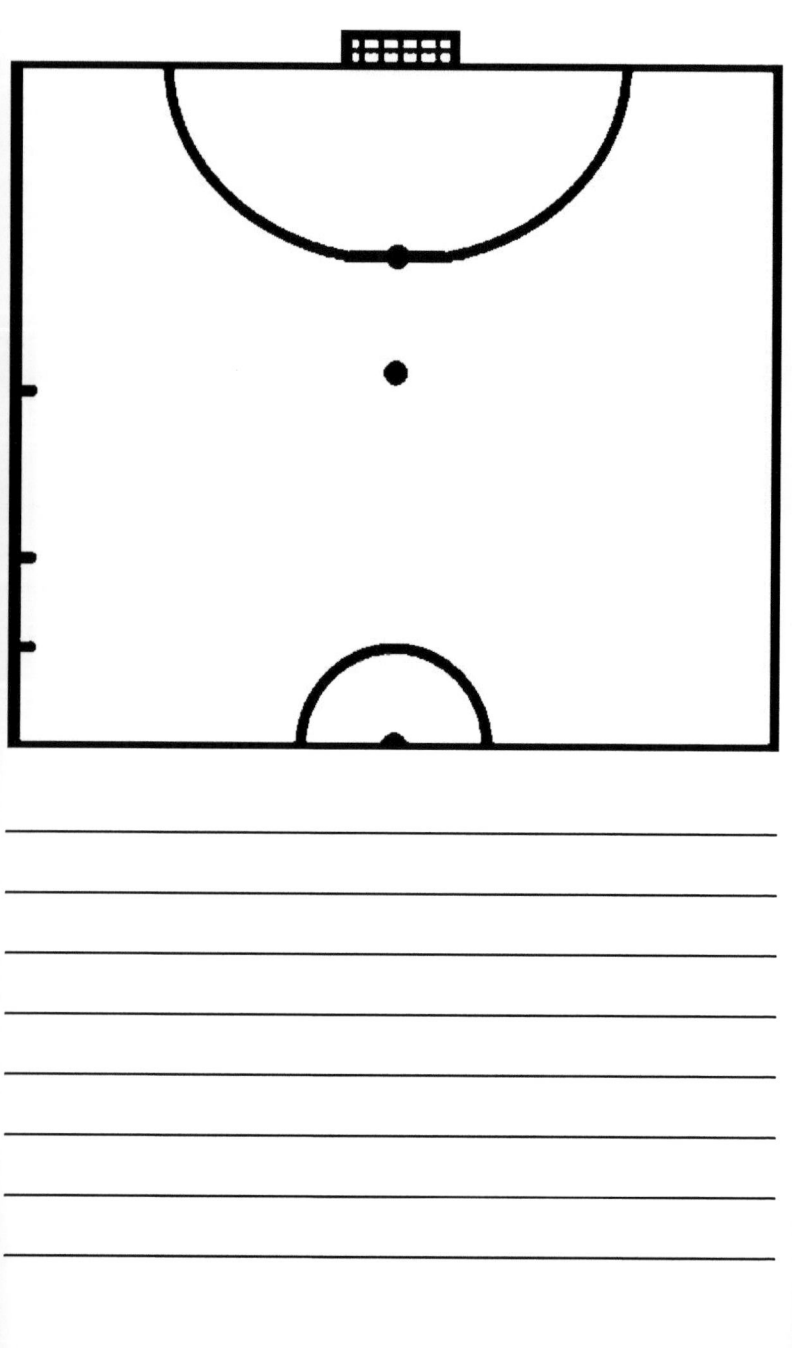

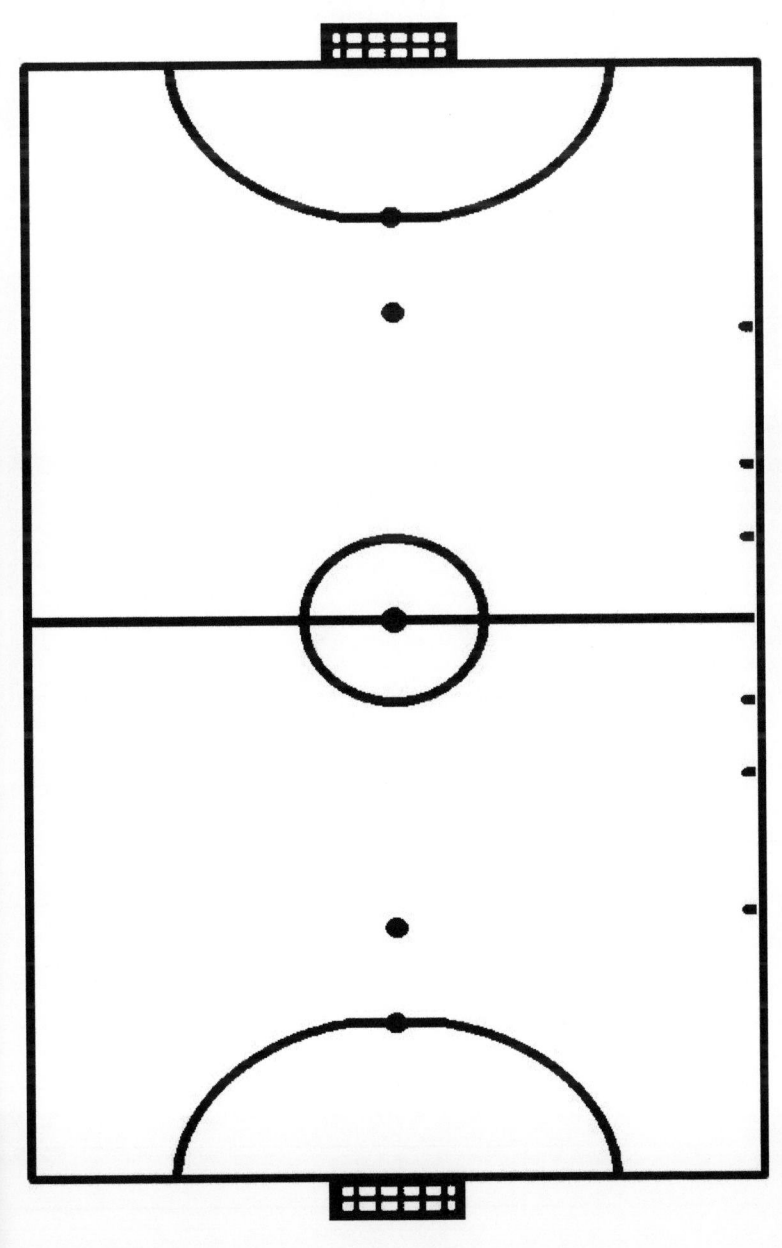

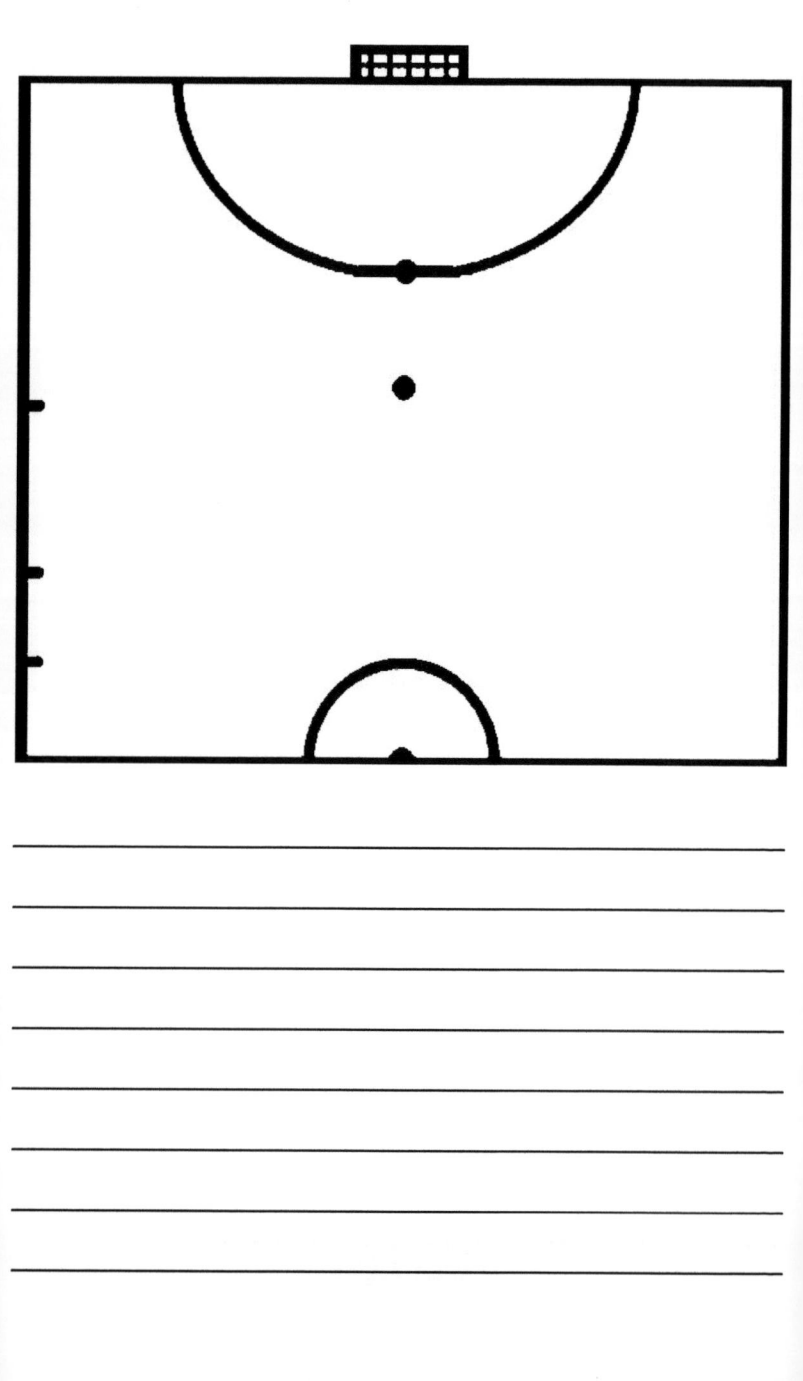

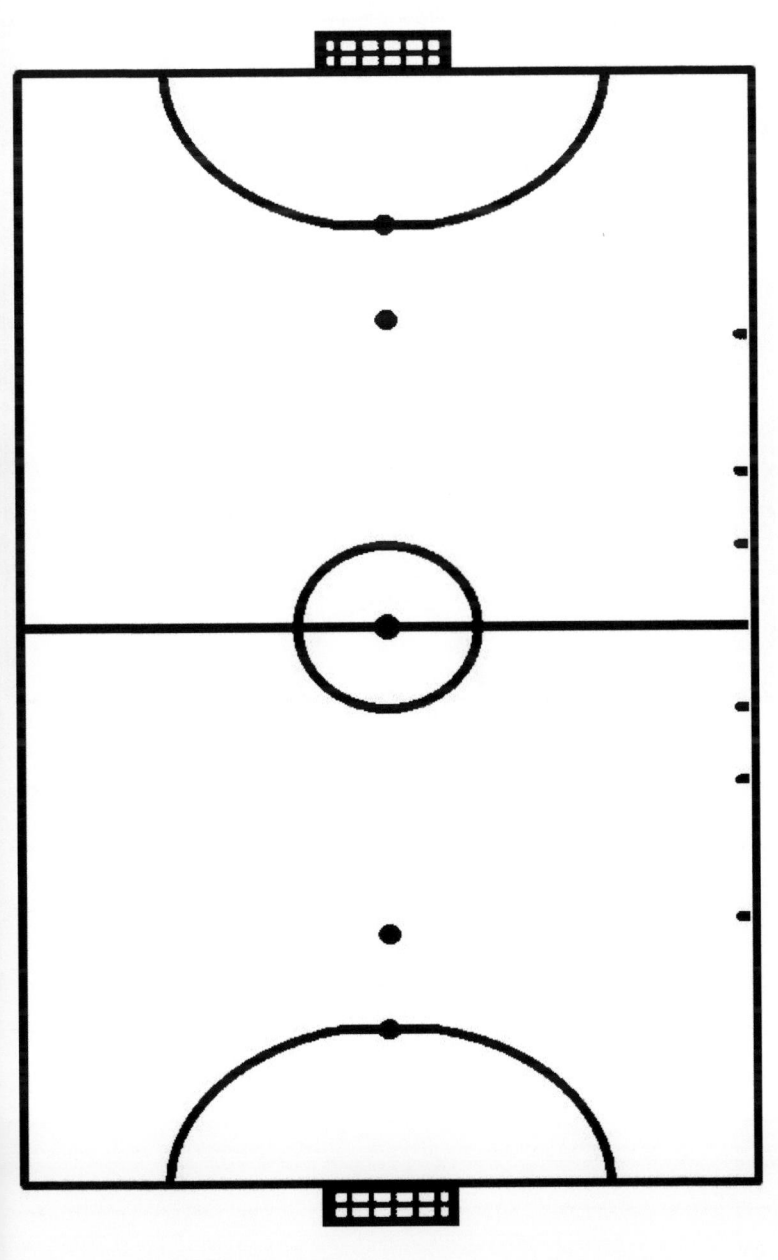

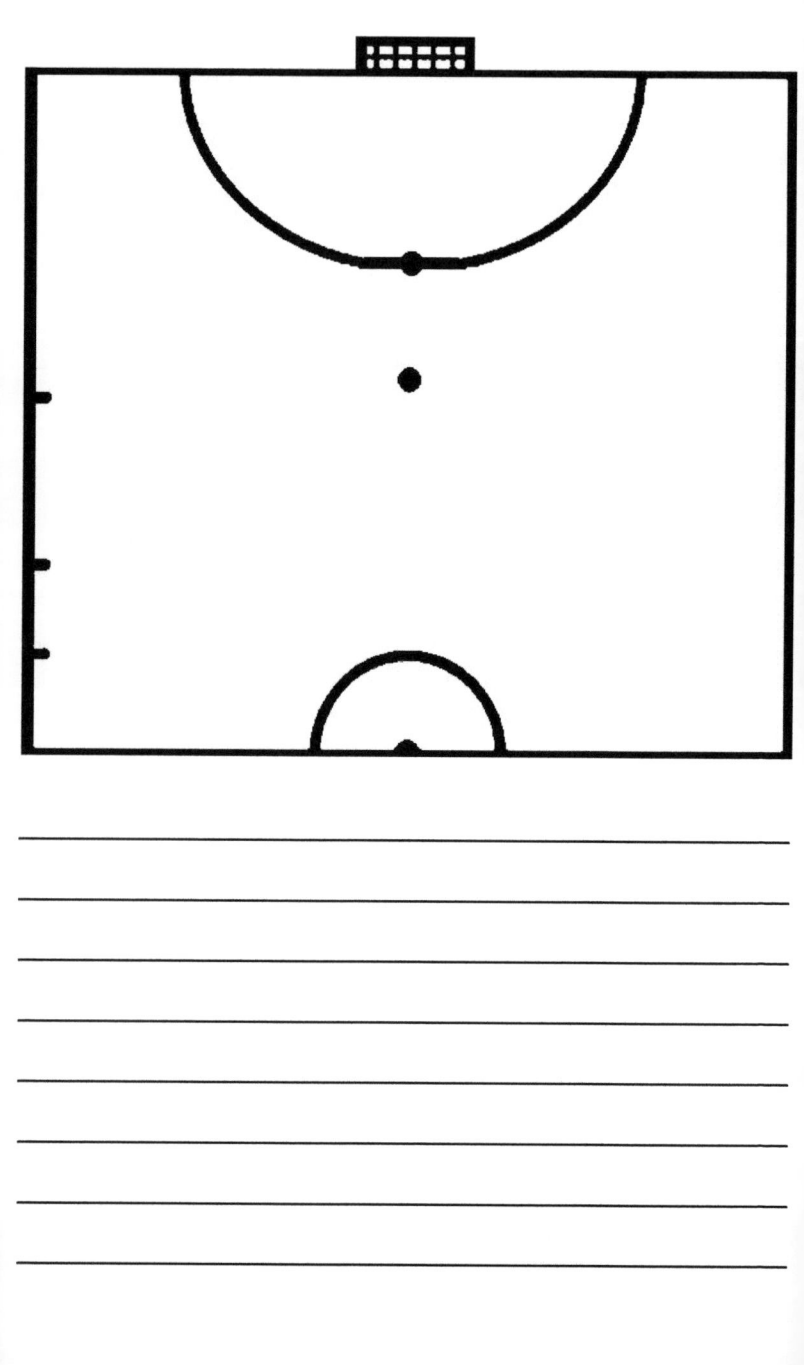

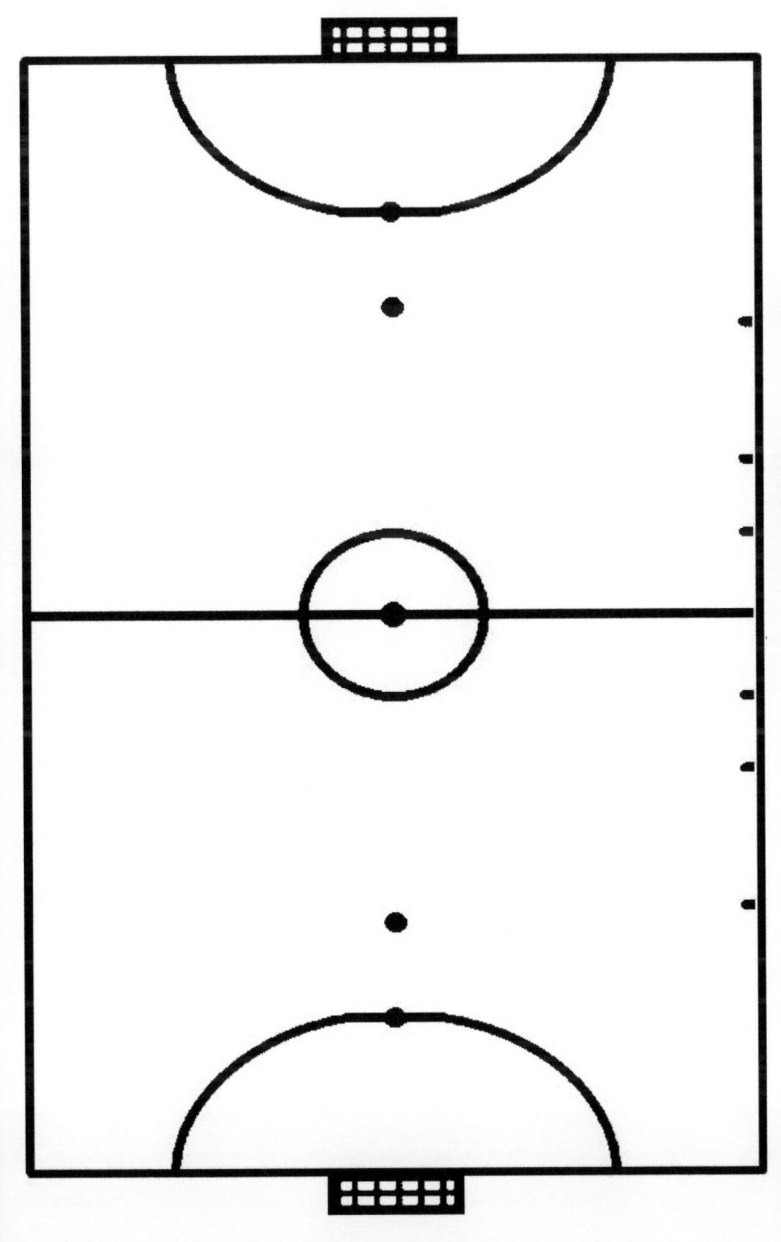

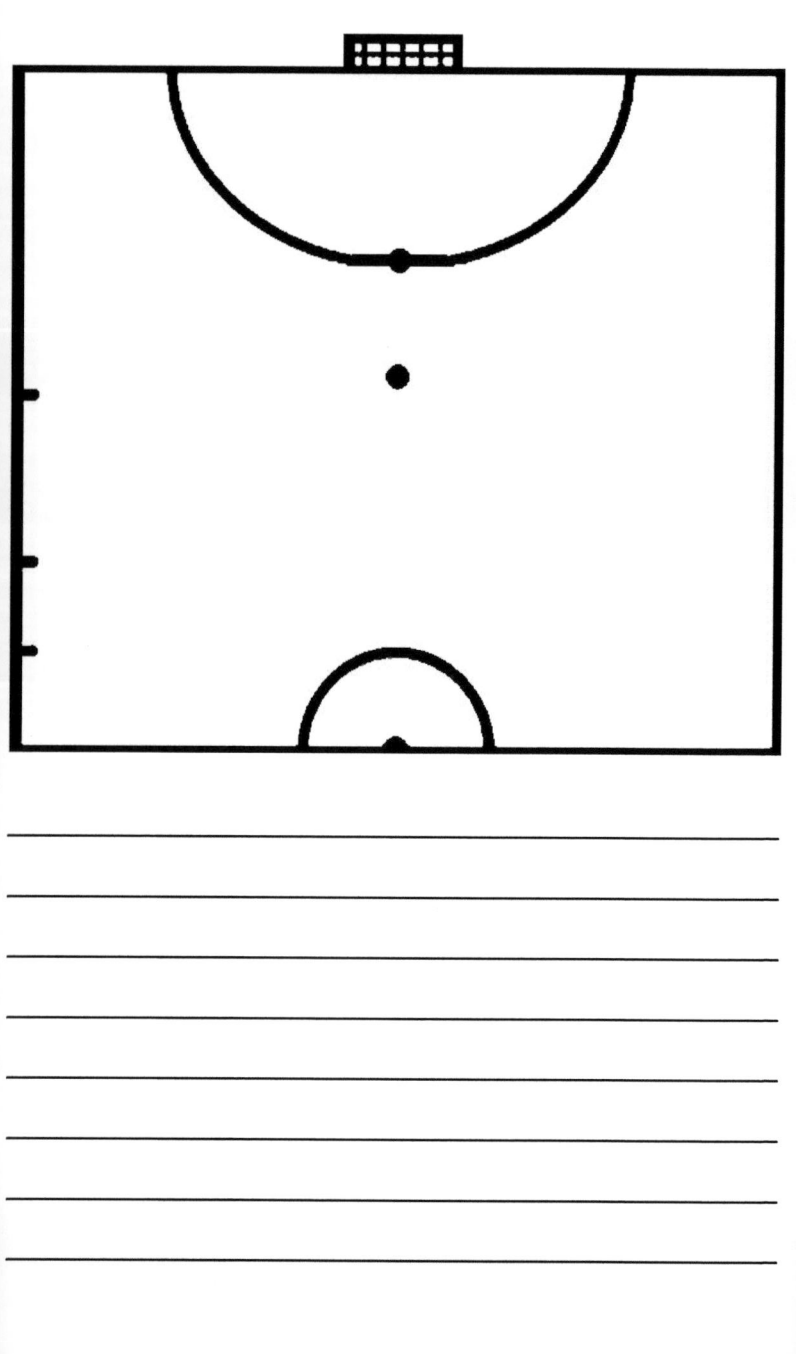

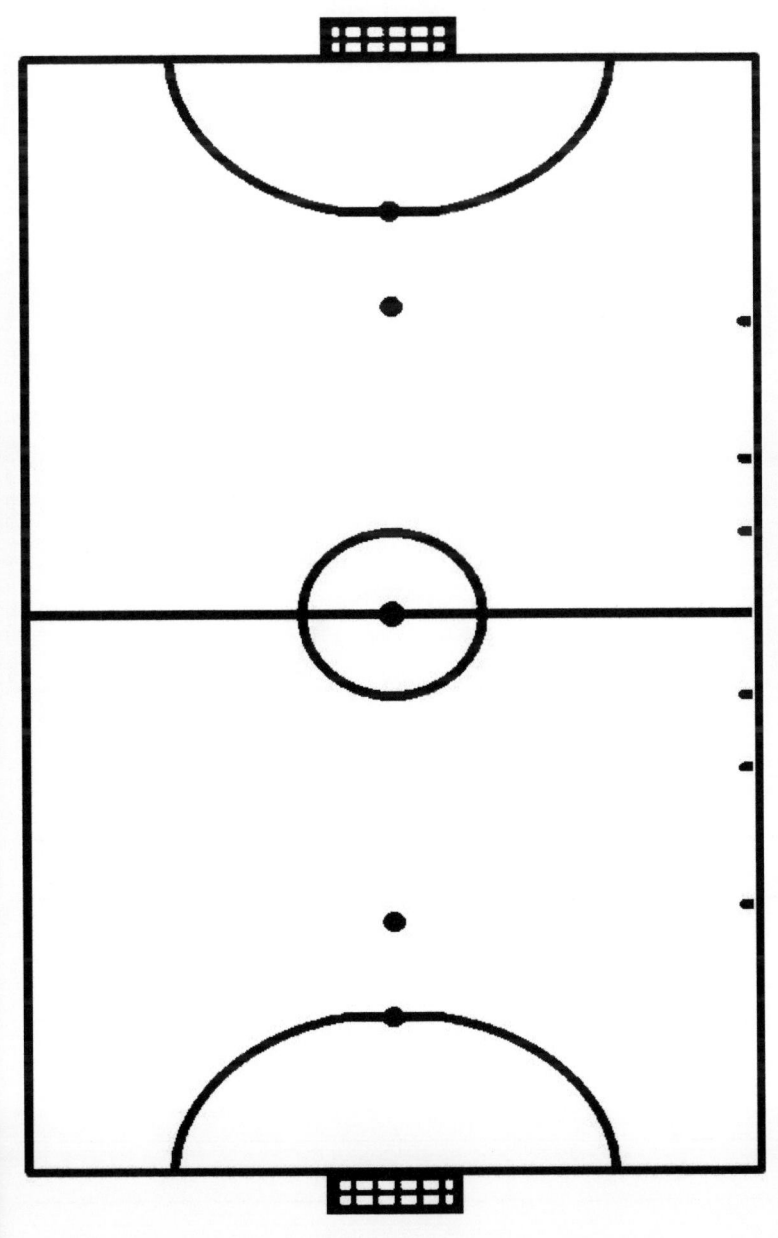

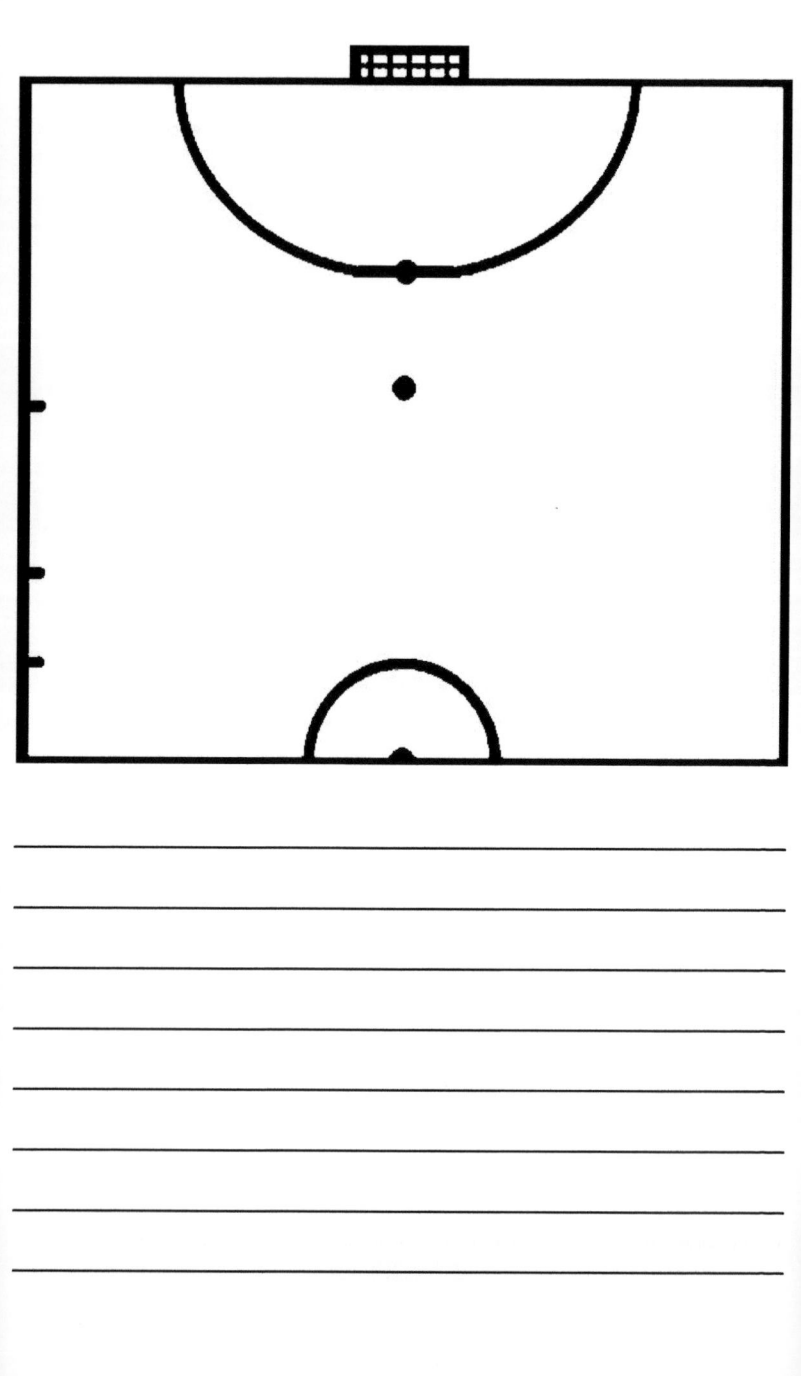

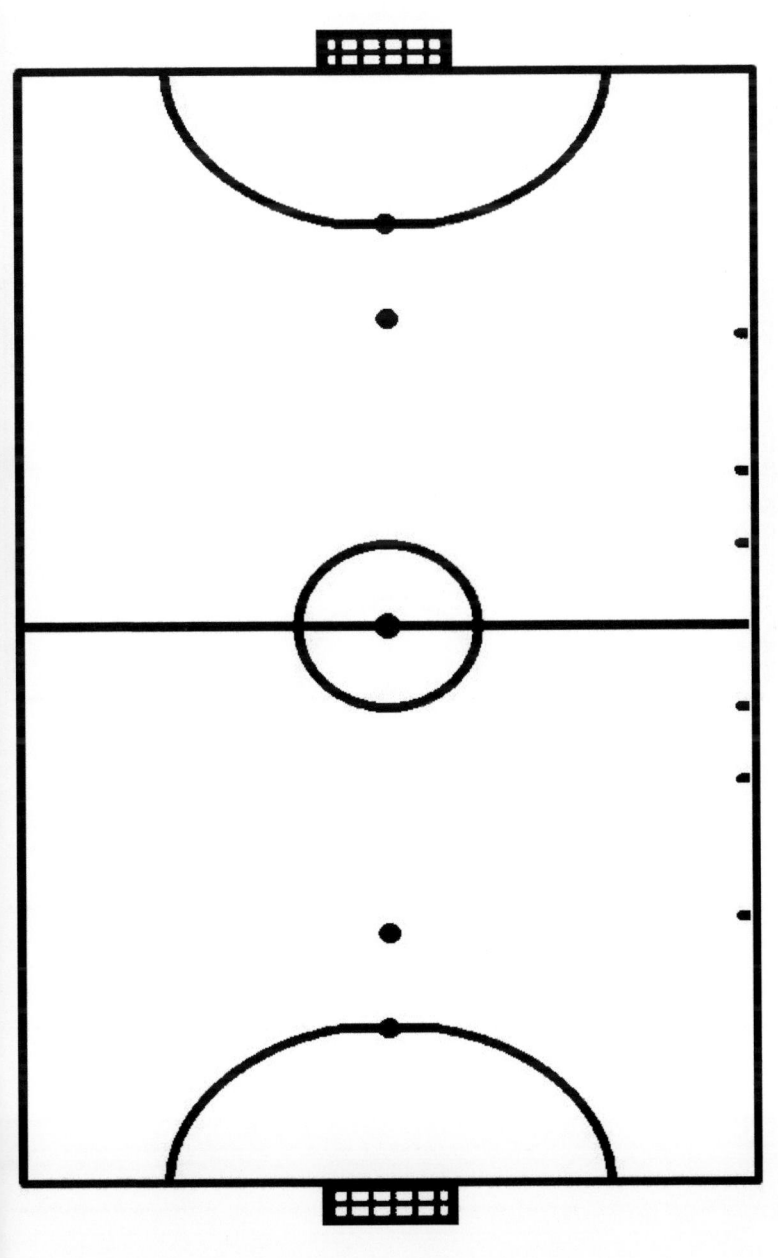

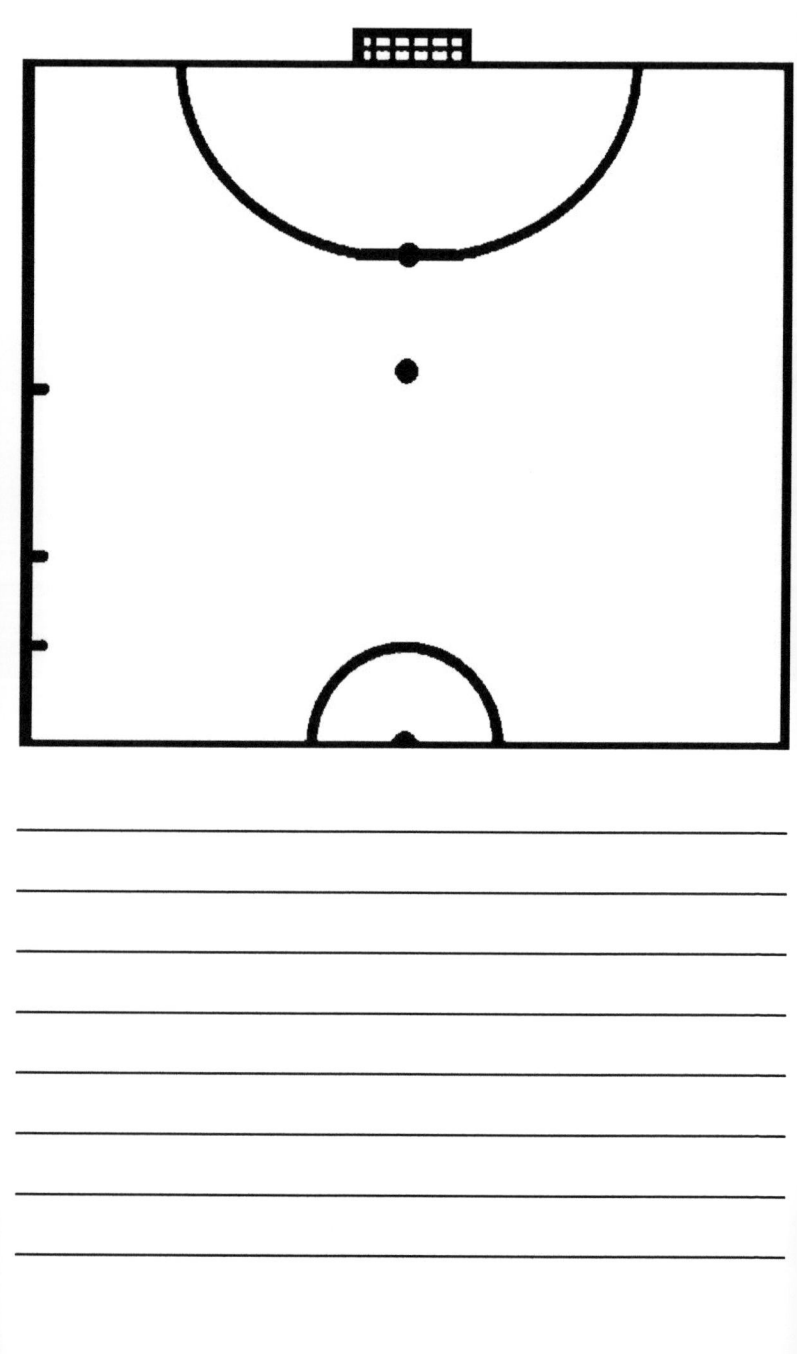

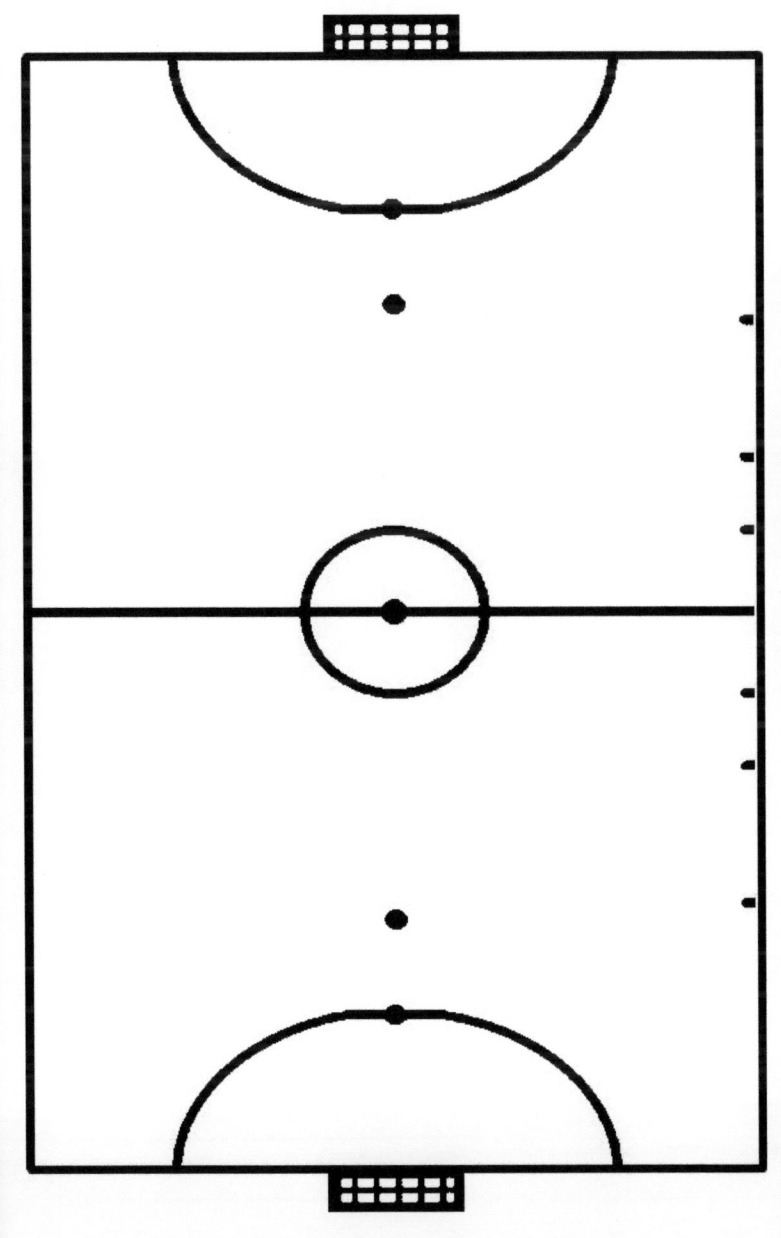

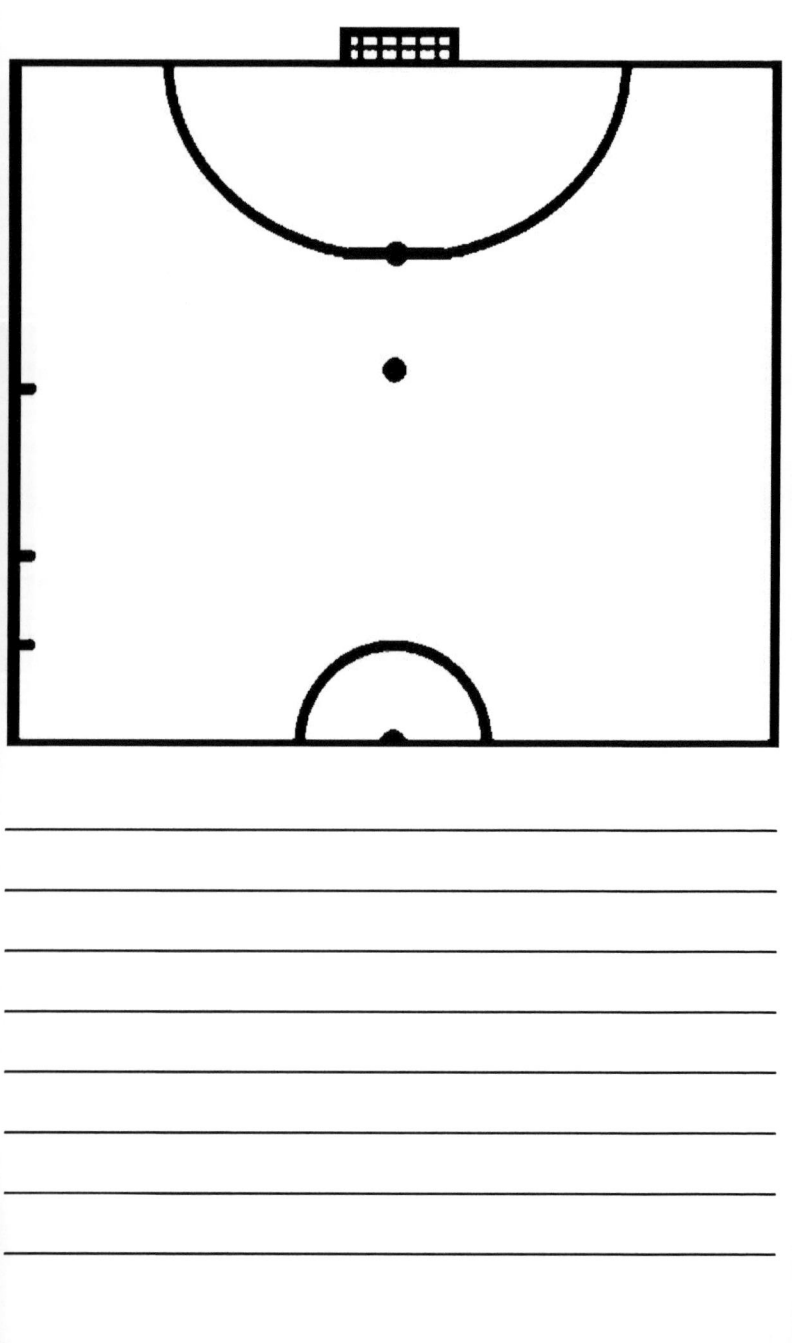

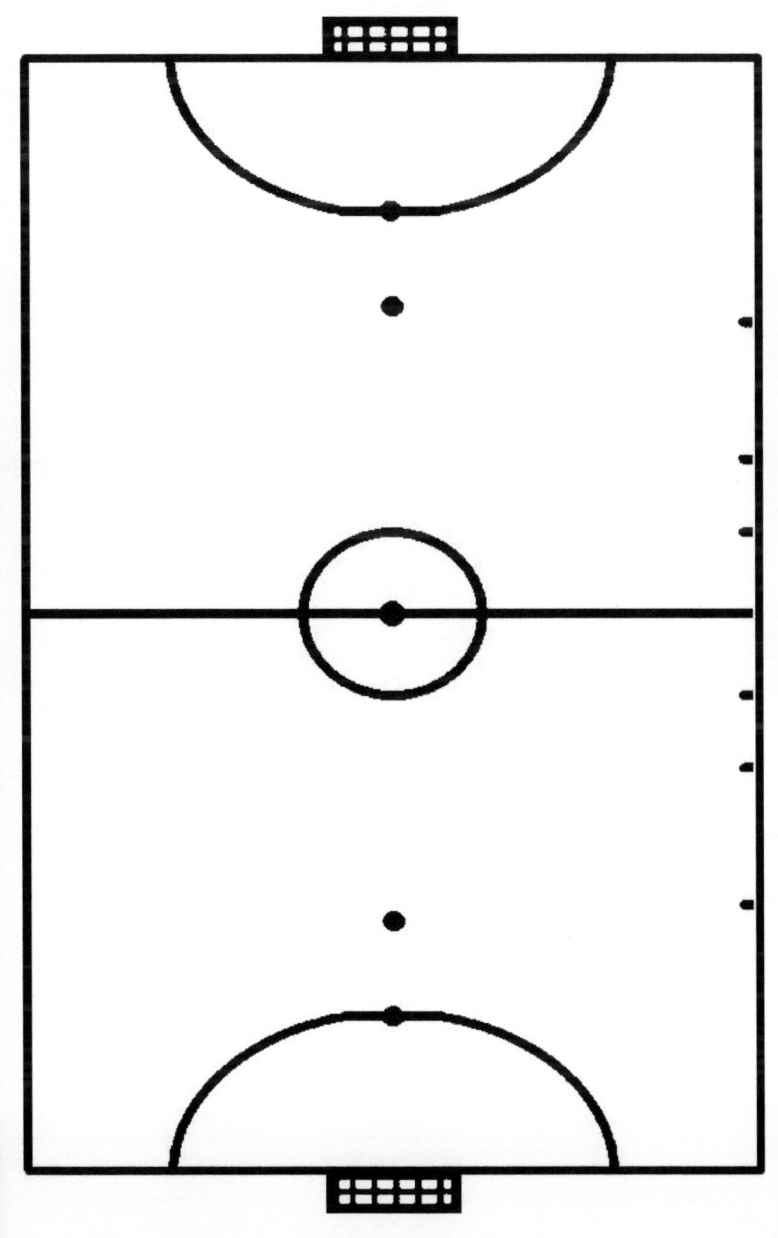

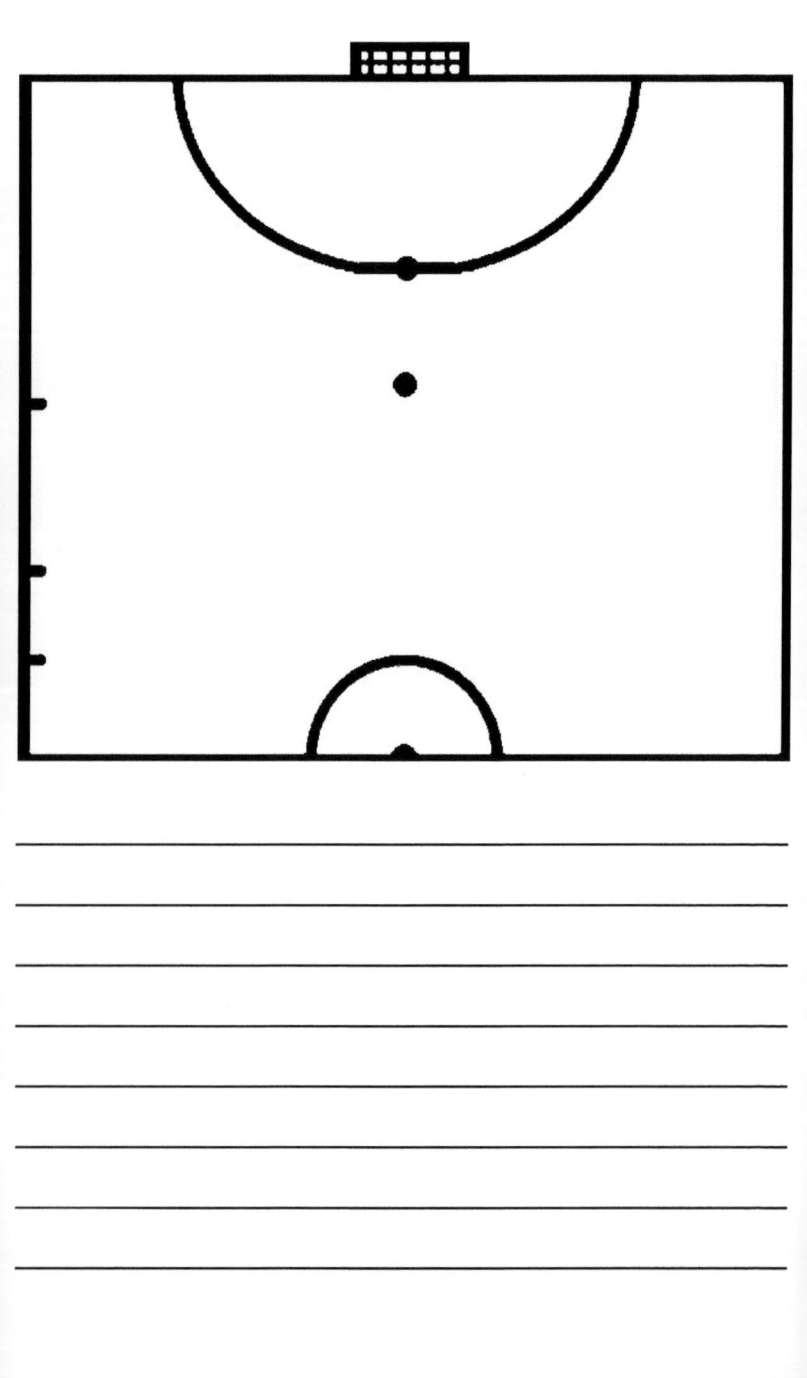

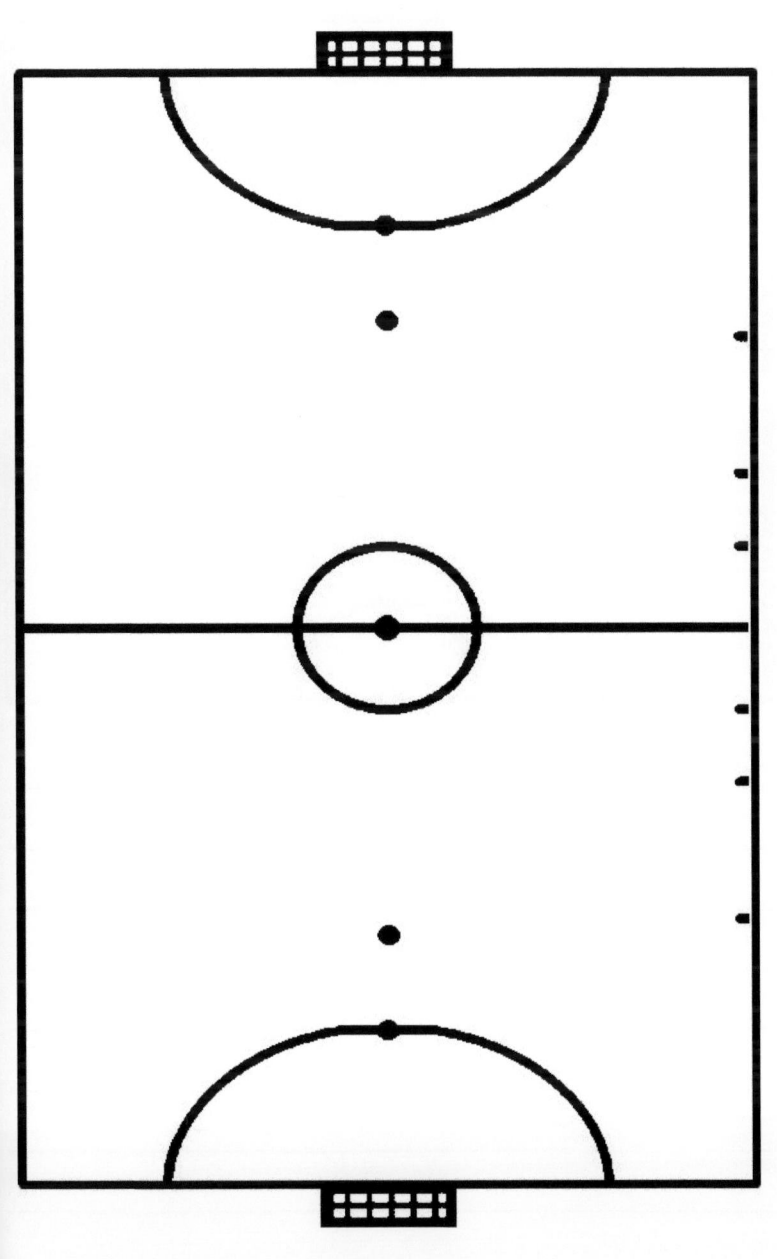

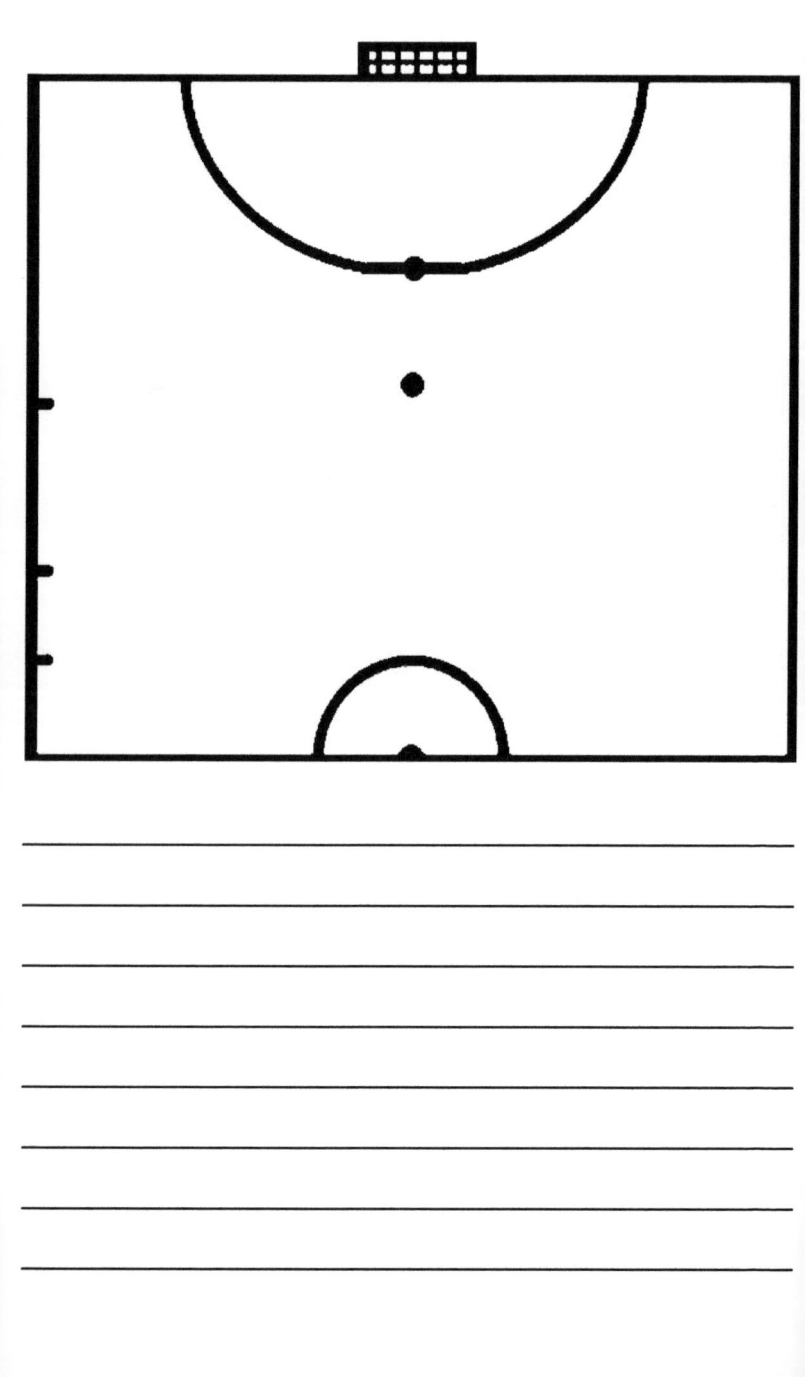

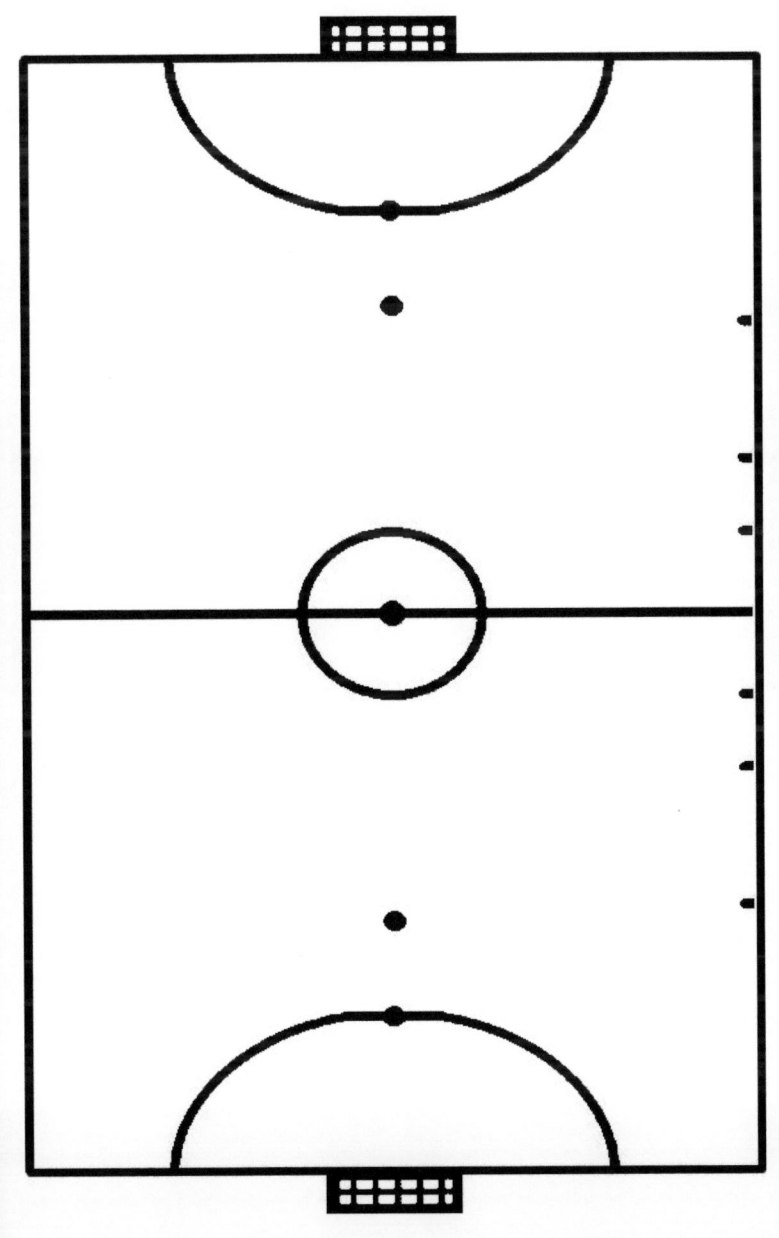

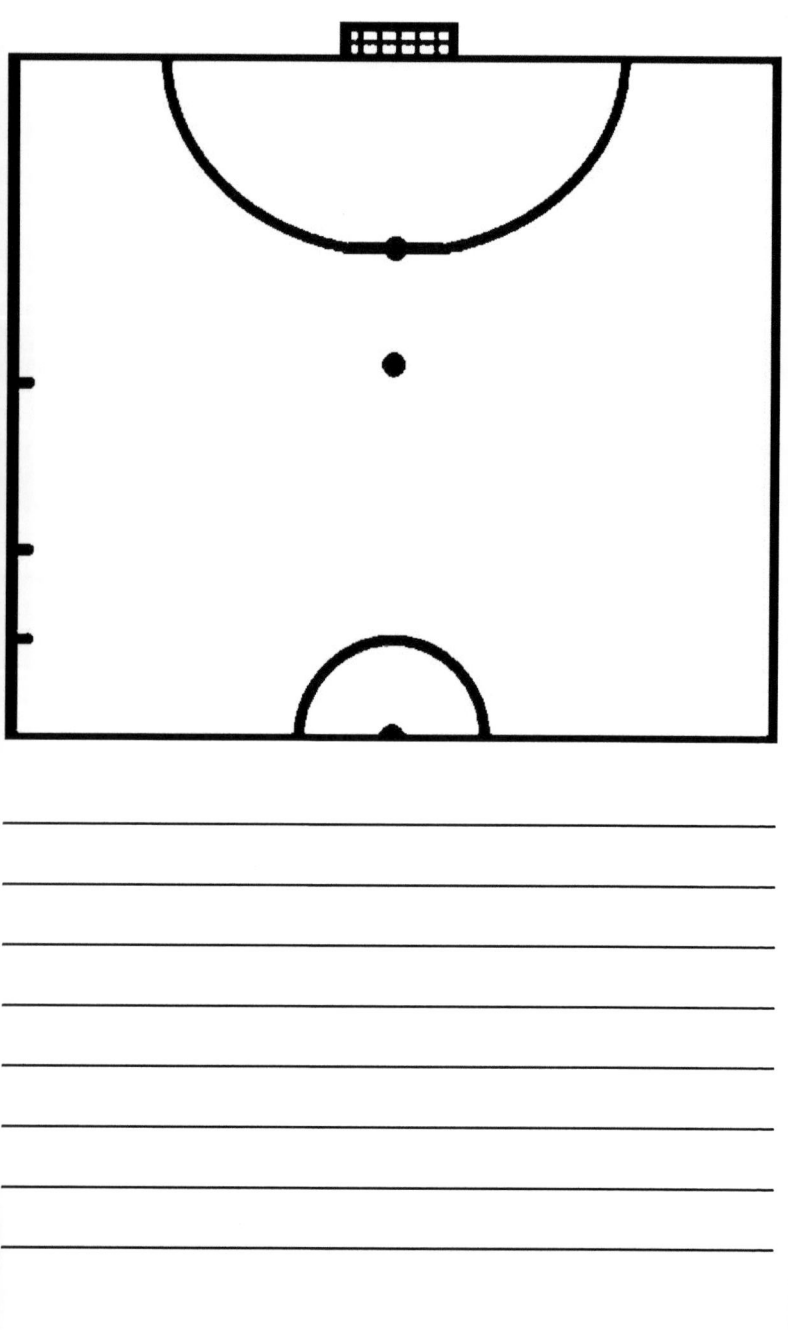

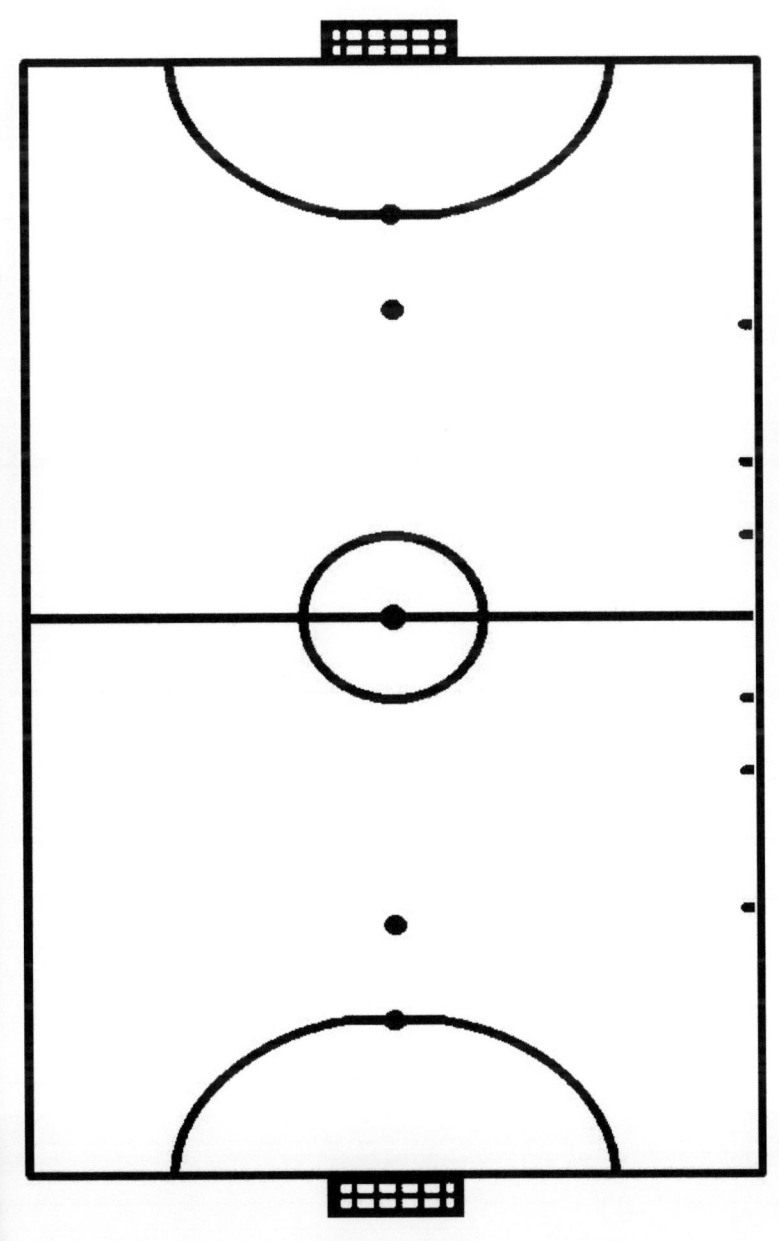

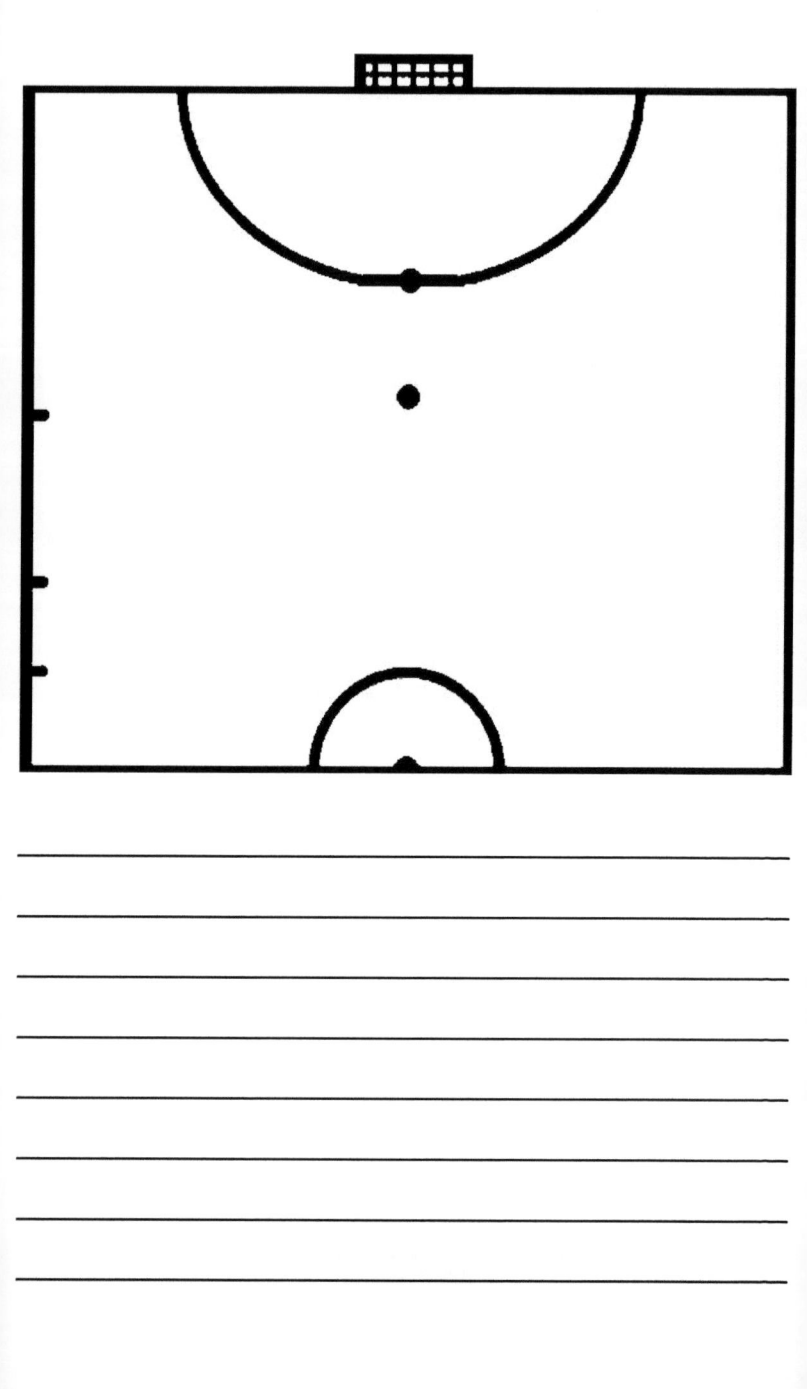

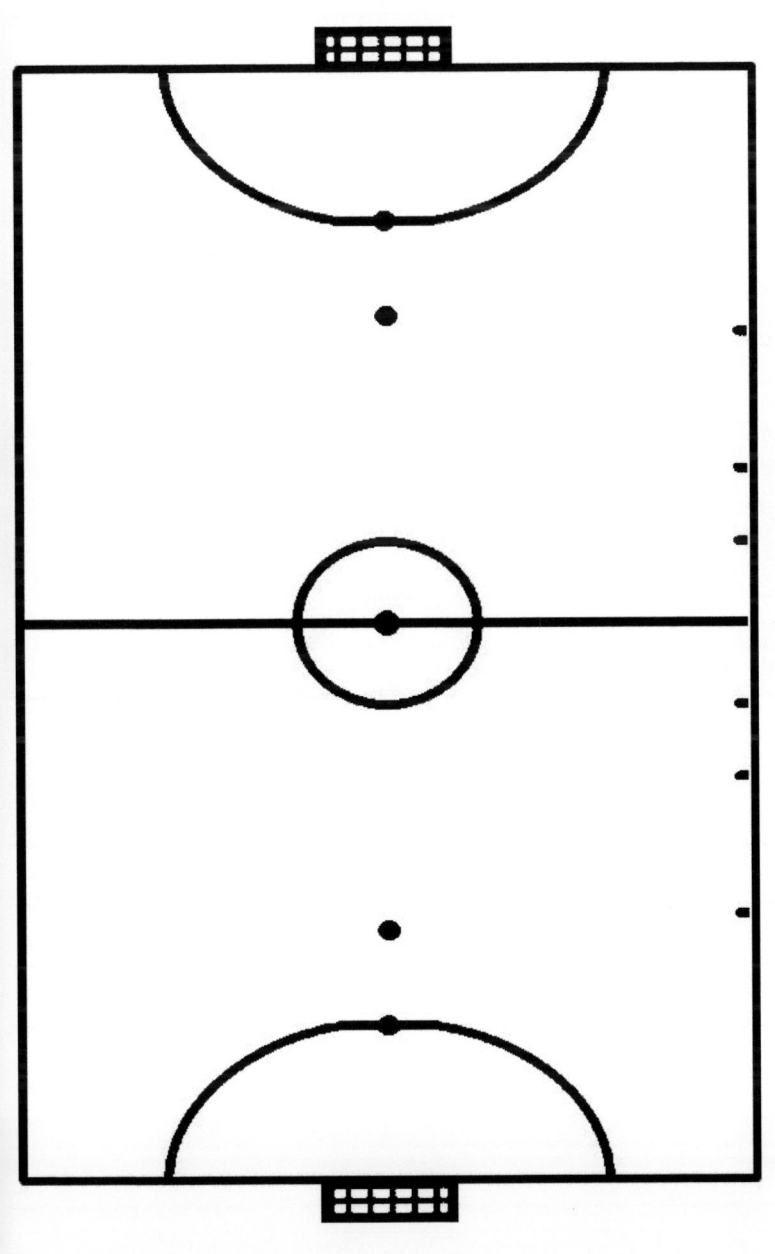

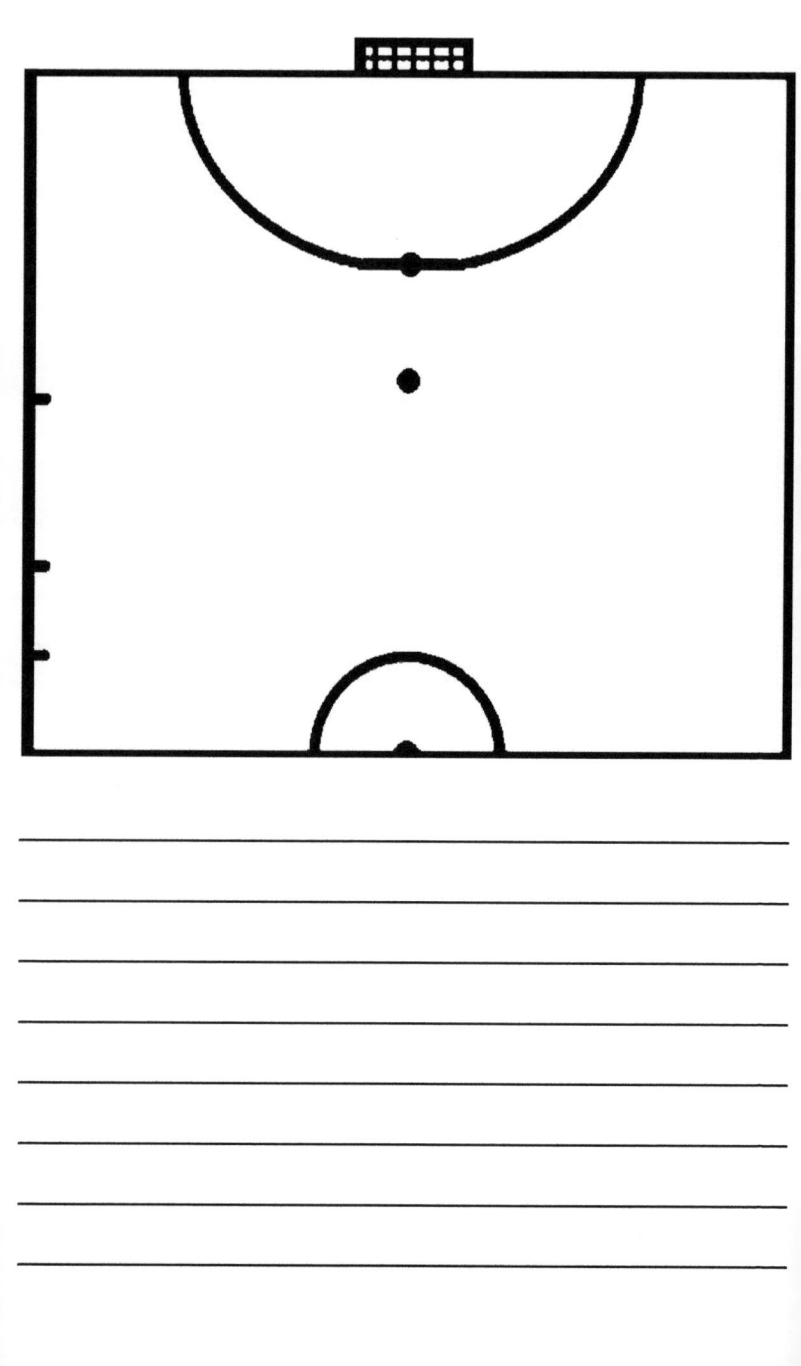

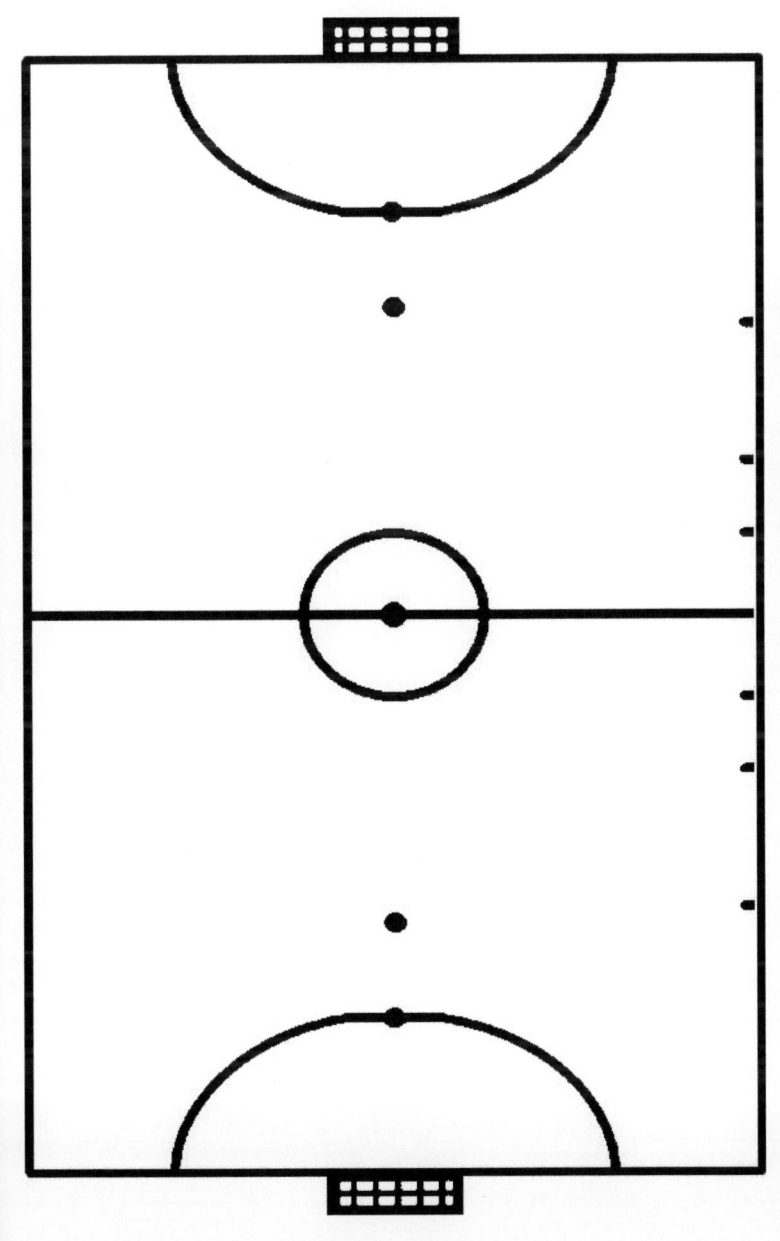

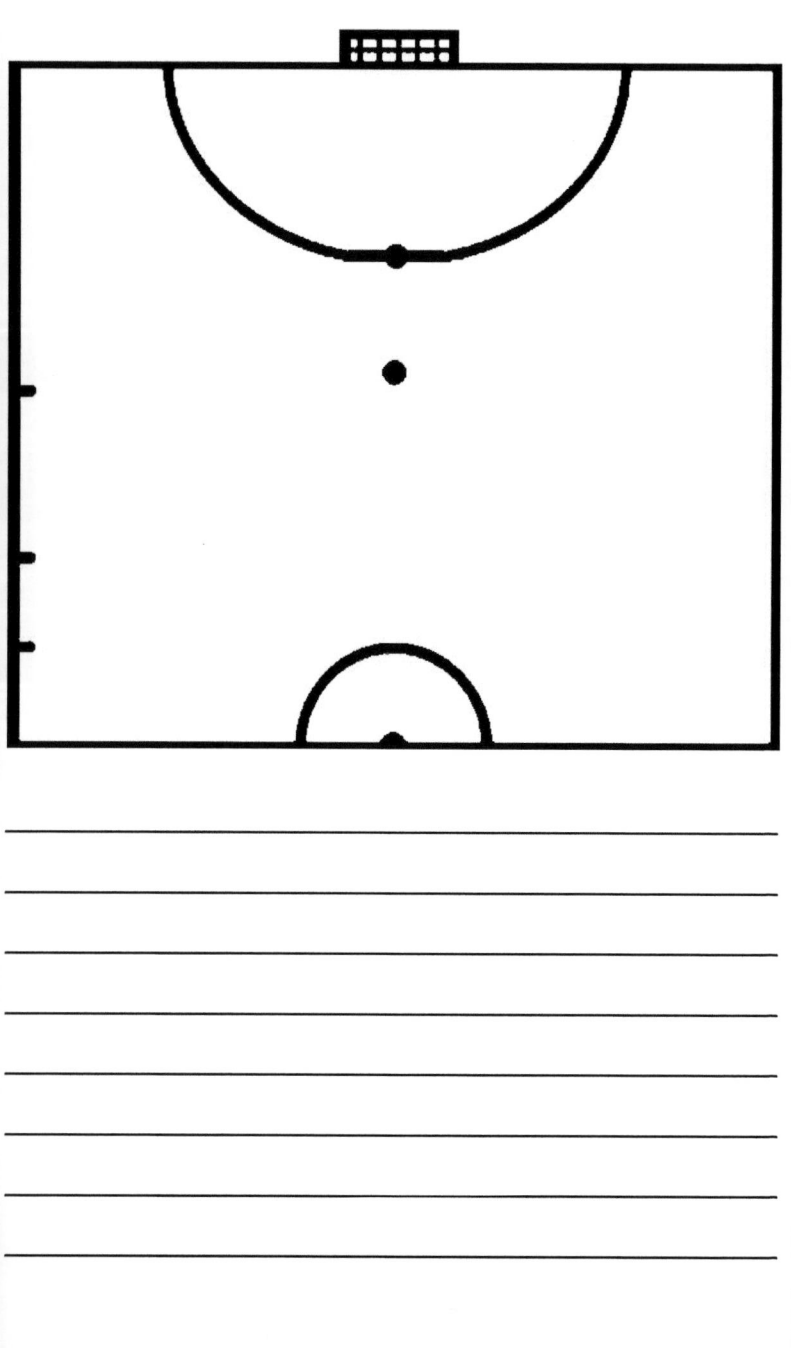

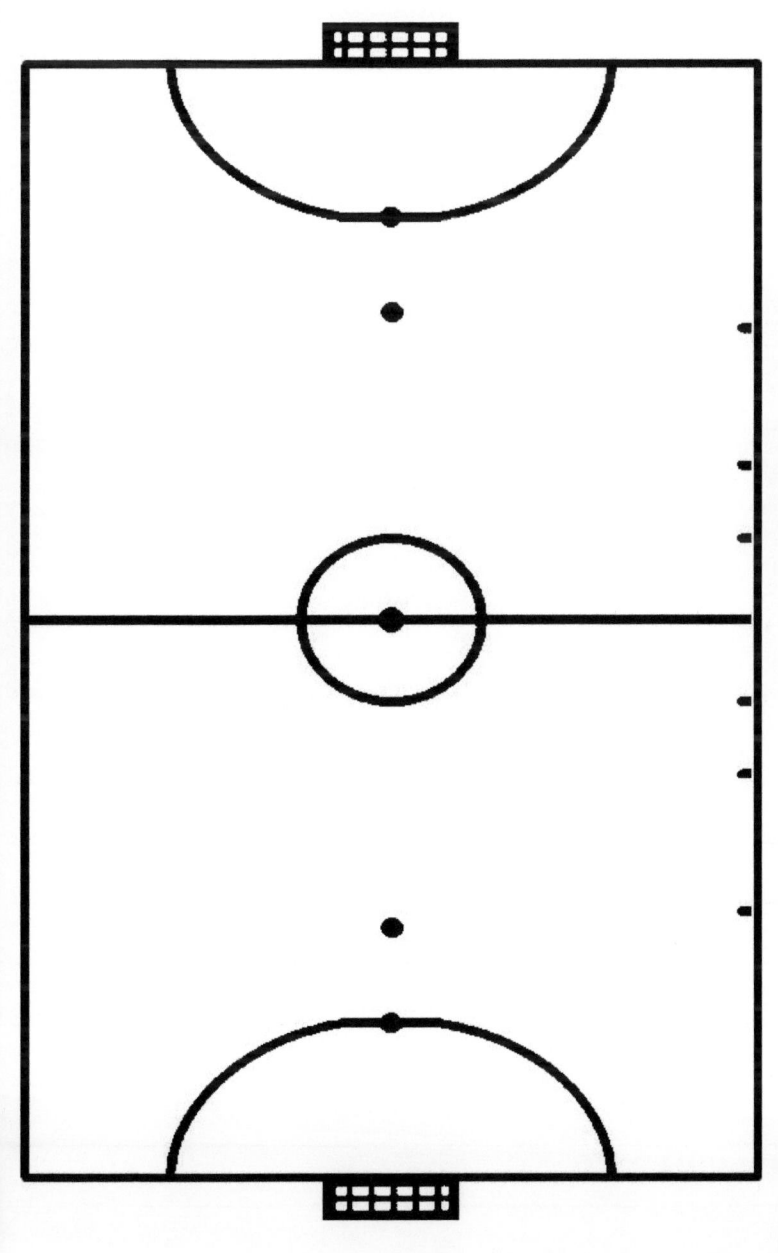

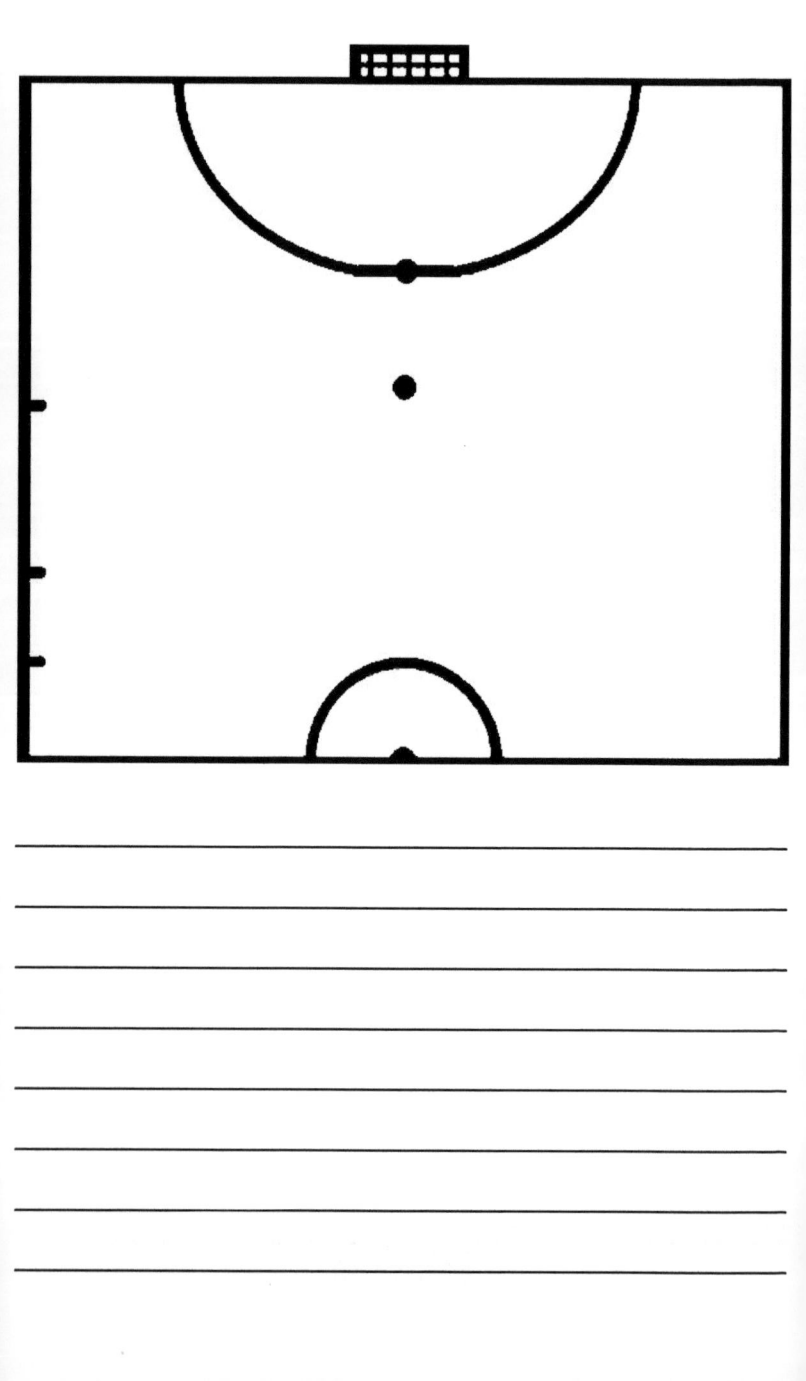

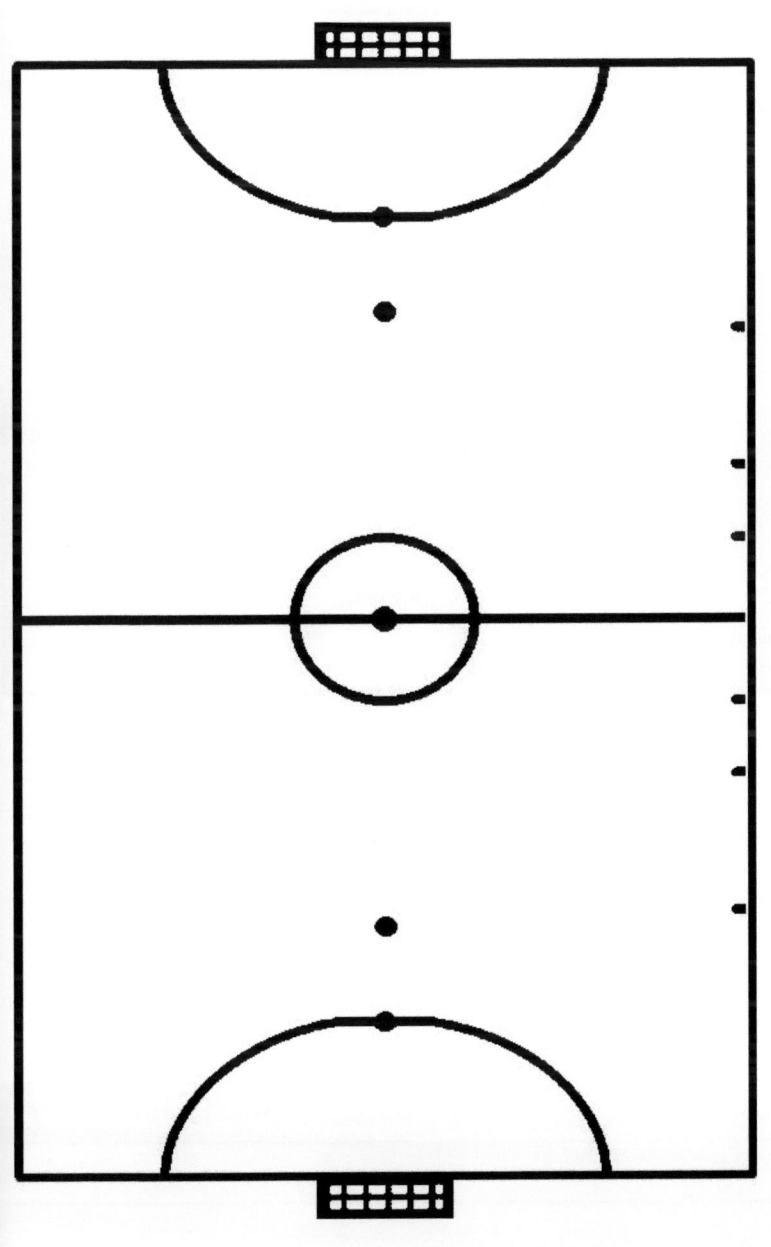

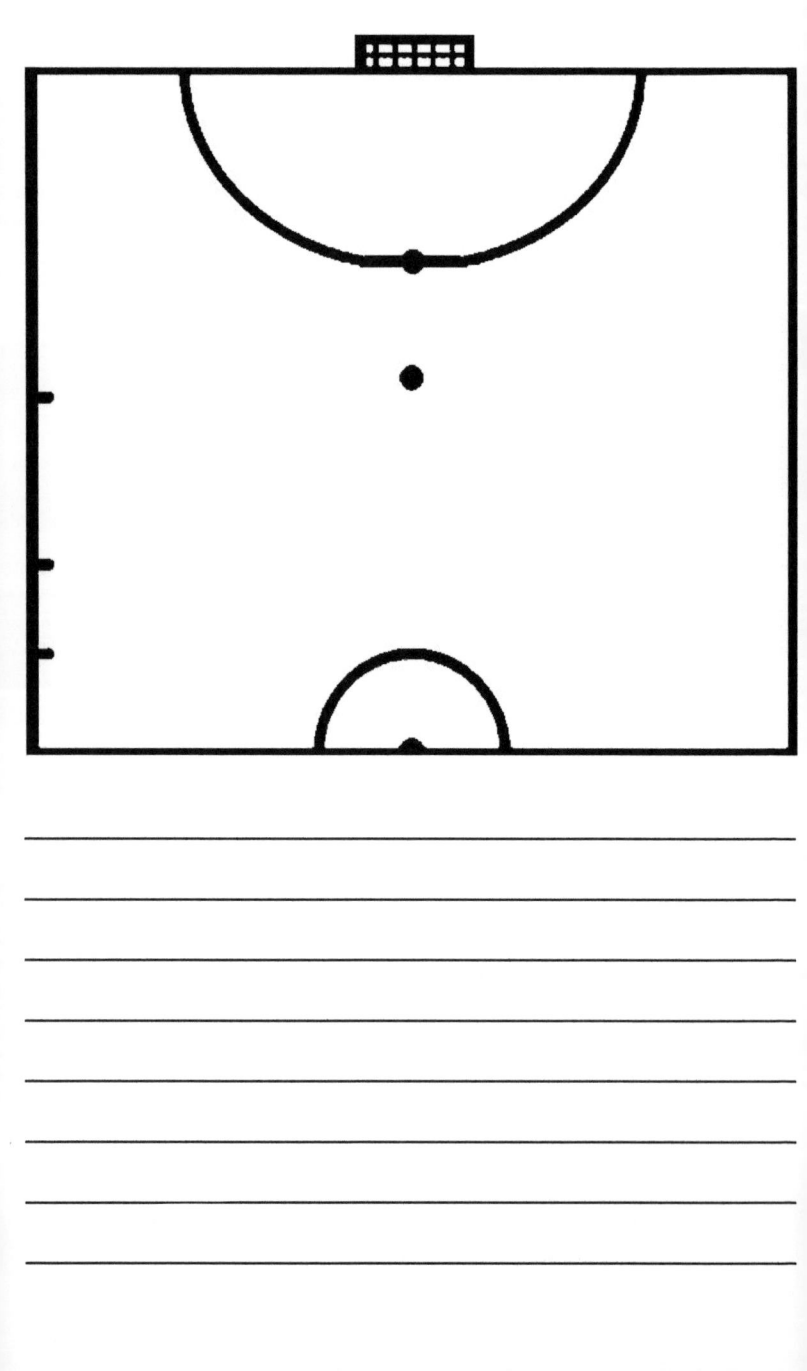

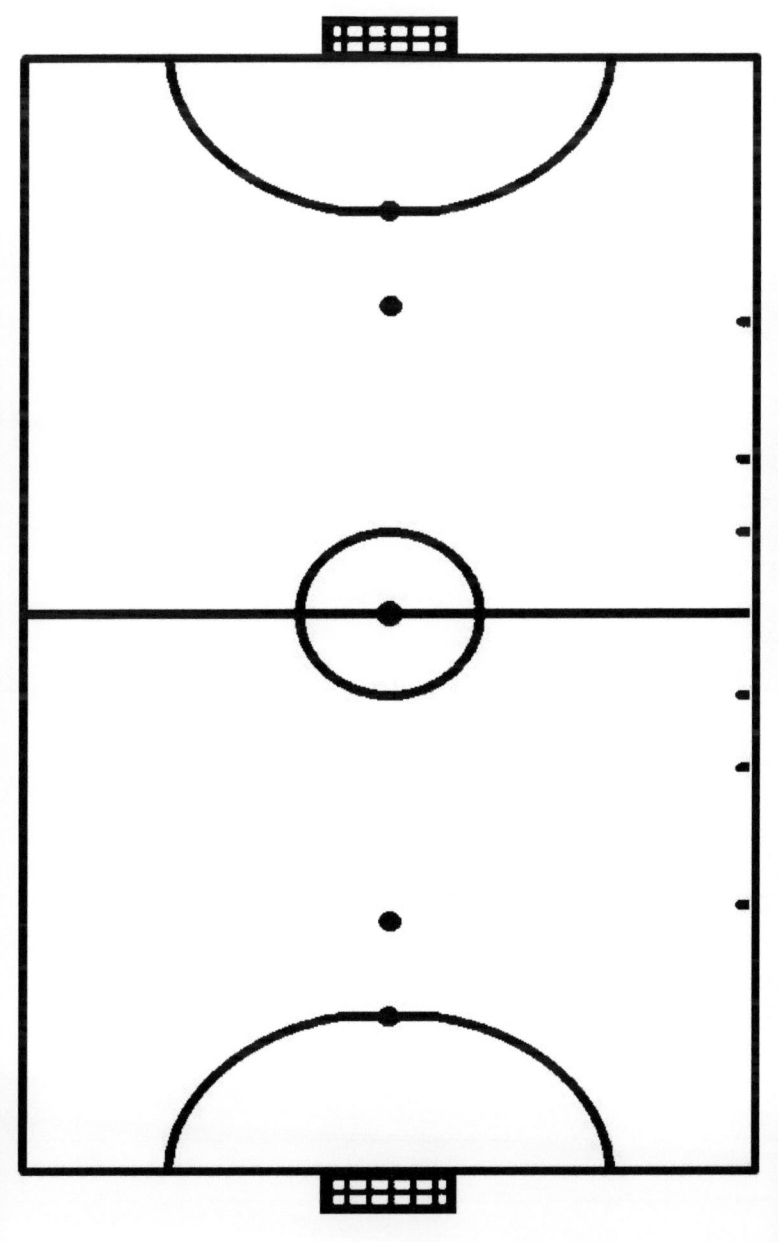

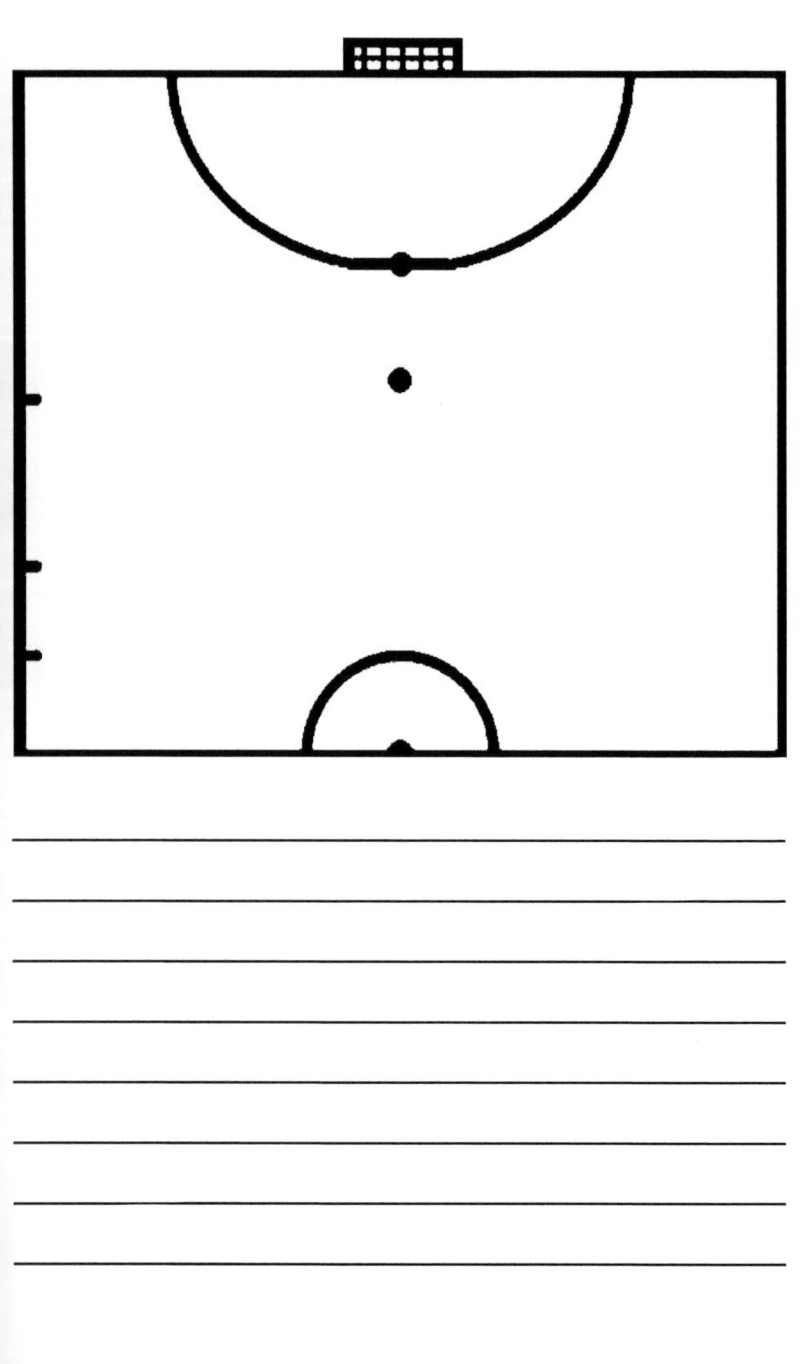

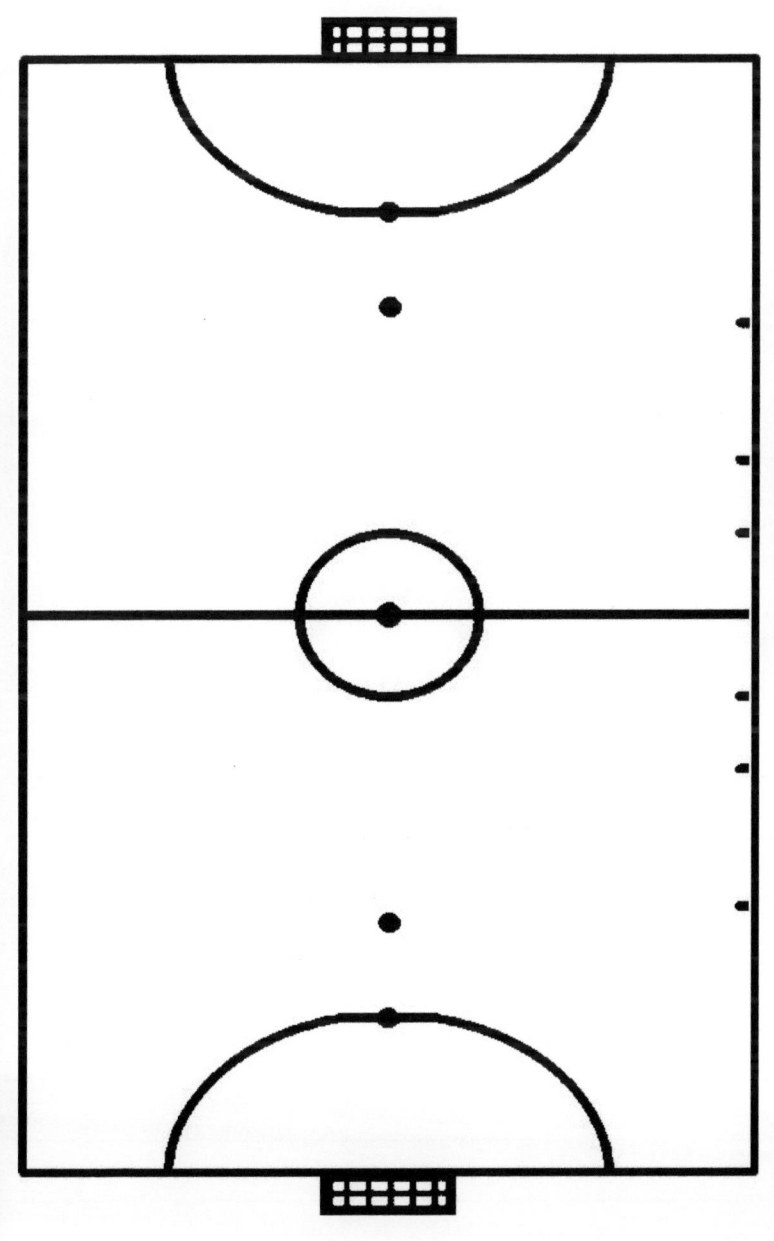

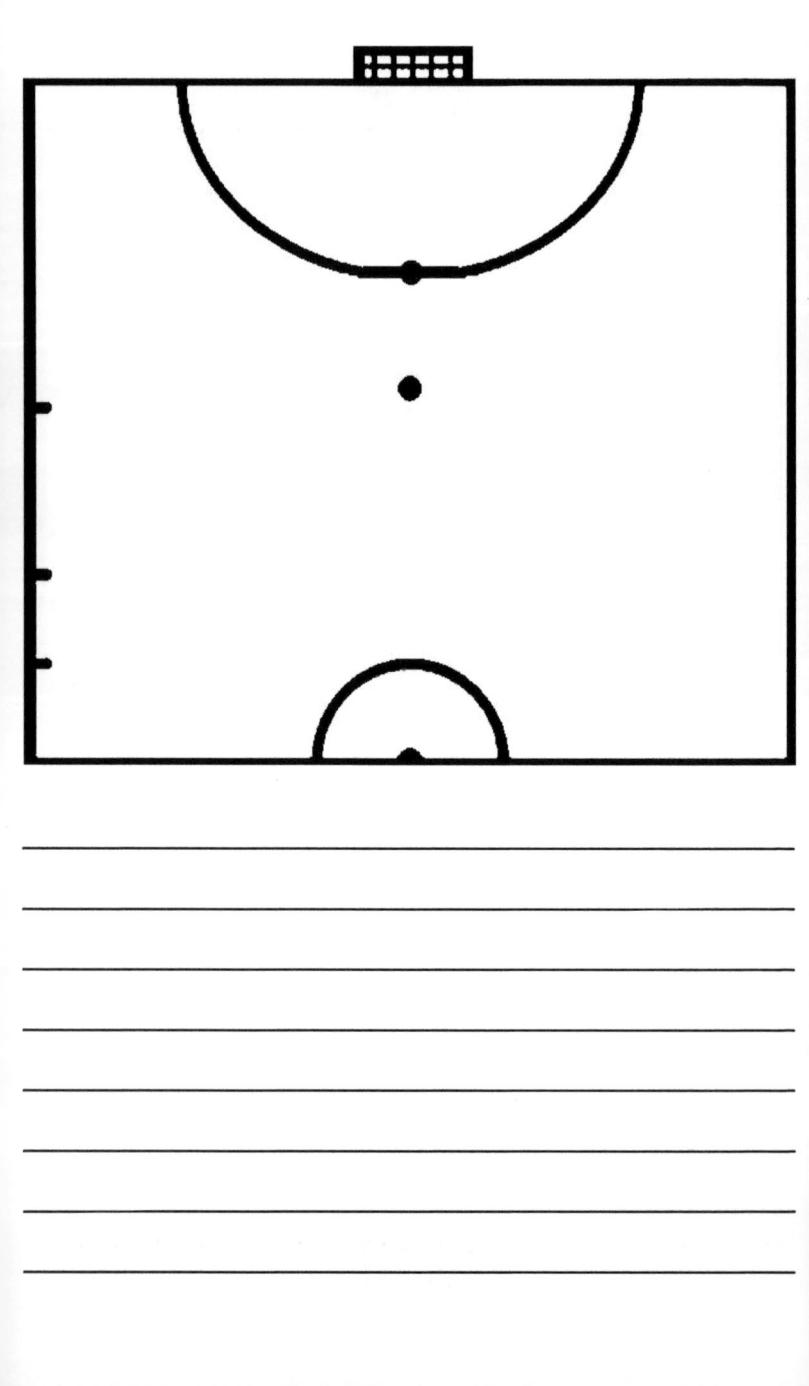

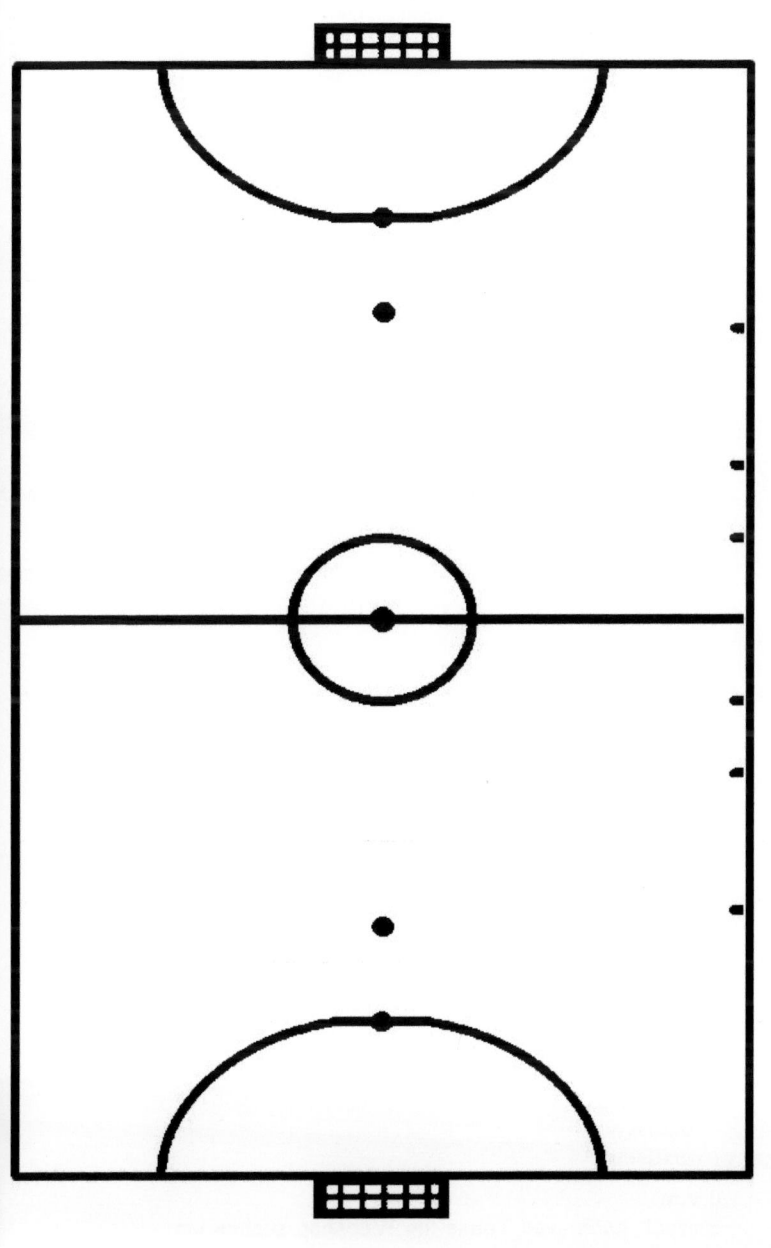

Weitere Bücher von Theo von Taane

- Happy – Wünsch dir was! ISBN: 9783734728570
- Tennis Witze Knallbonbons ISBN: 9783732296490
- Tennis Postkarten Kalender ISBN: 9783734741289
- Witze rund um Volleyball ISBN: 9783734731801
- Witze rund um Basketball ISBN: 9783734703824
- Witze rund ums Schwimmen ISBN: 9783734734460
- Witze rund um Schach ISBN: 9783734731658
- Witze rund um Tischtennis ISBN: 9783734731648
- Witze rund um Eishockey ISBN: 9783734730716
- Witze rund ums Fechten ISBN: 9783734731976
- Witze rund um Handball ISBN: 9783734731690
- Witze rund um Badminton ISBN: 9783734732875
- Witze rund um Karate ISBN: 9783734731666
- Witze rund um Judo ISBN: 9783734731674
- Witze rund um Golf ISBN: 9783734731704
- Witze rund um Fußball ISBN: 9783734731712

u.s.w.

Von Theo von Taane gibt es auch viele Rätsel-, Witze- , Spiele-, Ausmal- und Notizbüche Bücher zum Thema MINECRAFT.

Des Weiteren bietet Theo von Taane Taktikboard und Trainingsbücher auch zu folgende Sportarten an:

- Badminton
- Baseball
- Basketball
- Bowling
- Cricket
- Eishockey
- Fechten
- Feldhockey
- Fußball
- Futsal
- Handball
- Lacrosse (w)
- Lacrosse (m)
- Netball
- Rugby
- Schach
- Squash
- Tennis
- Tischtennis
- Volleyball
- Wasserball

u.v.m.

Einfach nach ‚von Taane' im Webshop suchen um sich die mehr als 200 Theo von Taane Bücher anzeigen zu lassen.

Theo von Taane

3D Rugby 2 in 1
Tacticboard & Training Workbook

The 2 in 1 Tacticboard & Training Workbook for fast creation of coaching instructions/game tactics and schemes, doesn't only offer sport specific preprints (playing field and space for notes), but also a cover, usable as a dry erase panel (whiteboard pen is needed).

ADVANTAGES:

o notebook with sport specific preprints (playing field) for fast and simple sketching of coaching instructions/game tactics and schemes

o If all pages of the notebook are used, the cover is still a dry erase panel (tacticboard)

o Due to a handy format, the notebook can be comfortably used in any situation (e.g. on the way or on the playing field)

o Perfect for spontaneous collection of ideas or as a memorization tool

o Practical handling due to easy pocket format

Bibliografische Information der Deutschen Nationalbibliothek:
Die Deutsche Nationalbibliothek verzeichnet diese Publikation in der Deutschen Nationalbibliografie; detaillierte bibliografische Daten sind im Internet über http://dnb.dnb.de abrufbar.

© 2016 Theo von Taane; 1. Auflage

Texte und Illustrationen: **Theo von Taane**

Herstellung und Verlag: BoD – Books on Demand, Norderstedt

ISBN: 9783739233314